CONFIGURING INVENTORY MANAGEMENT WITHIN DYNAMICS 365 FOR FINANCE & OPERATIONS

MODULE 5: CONFIGURING BATCH AND SERIALIZED PRODUCTS

MURRAY FIFE

ISBN-13: 978-1078175852

Preface

What You Need for this Guide

All the examples shown in this blueprint were done with the Microsoft Dynamics 365 for Operations hosted image that was provisioned through Lifecycle Services.

The following list of software from the virtual image was leveraged within this guide:

Microsoft Dynamics 365 for Operations

Even though all the preceding software was used during the development and testing of the recipes in this book, they should also work on later versions without any changes.

Errata

Although we have taken every care to ensure the accuracy of our content, mistakes do happen. If you find a mistake in one of our books—maybe a mistake in the text or the code—we would be grateful if you would report this to us. By doing so, you can save other readers from frustration and help us improve subsequent versions of this book. If you find any errata, please report them by emailing editor@dynamicscompanions.com.

Piracy

Piracy of copyright material on the Internet is an ongoing problem across all media. If you come across any illegal copies of our works, in any form, on the Internet, please provide us with the location address or website name immediately so that we can pursue a remedy.

Please contact us at legal@dynamicscompanions.com with a link to the suspected pirated material.

We appreciate your help in protecting our authors, and our ability to bring you valuable content.

Questions

You can contact us at help@dynamicscompanions.com if you are having a problem with any aspect of the book, and we will do our best to address it.

Table of Contents

DYNAMICS COMPANIONS
BARE BONES CONFIGURATION GUIDE

CONFIGURING INVENTORY MANAGEMENT WITHIN DYNAMICS 365 FOR FINANCE & OPERATIONS
MODULE 5: CONFIGURING BATCH AND SERIALIZED PRODUCTS

Configuring Batched And Serialized Products

If you want you can also track your products by batch or serial number within Dynamics AX. These are just extra inventory dimensions that you enable on your products and give you that extra level of traceability when you look at your products.

In this section we will show you how to configure the batch and serial numbers and how to use them with products.

Topics Covered

- Configuring Number Groups

- Configuring A Batch Controlled Product

- Configuring A Serialized Product

- Summary

DYNAMICS COMPANIONS
BARE BONES CONFIGURATION GUIDE

CONFIGURING INVENTORY MANAGEMENT WITHIN DYNAMICS 365 FOR FINANCE & OPERATIONS
MODULE 5: CONFIGURING BATCH AND SERIALIZED PRODUCTS

Configuring Number Groups

Before we start though there is just one small setup step that we need to perform, and that is to set up some **Number Groups**. These are used to control how the batch and serial numbers are tracked against a product.

Topics Covered

- Opening the Tracking number groups maintenance form

- Creating a Batch Date Tracking number group

- Creating a Serial Tracking number group

 www.dynamicscompanions.com
Dynamics Companions

- 7 -

www.blindsquirrelpublishing.com
© 2019 Blind Squirrel Publishing, LLC , All Rights Reserved

 BLIND SQUIRREL
PUBLISHING

DYNAMICS COMPANIONS
BARE BONES CONFIGURATION GUIDE

CONFIGURING INVENTORY MANAGEMENT WITHIN DYNAMICS 365 FOR FINANCE & OPERATIONS
MODULE 5: CONFIGURING BATCH AND SERIALIZED PRODUCTS

Opening the Tracking number groups maintenance form

To do this we will need to open the **Tracking number groups** maintenance form.

How to do it...

Step 1: Open the Tracking number groups form through the menu

We can get to the **Tracking number groups** form a couple of different ways. The first way is through the master menu.

To do this, open up the navigation panel, expand out the **Modules** and group, and click on **Inventory management** to see all of the menu items that are available. Then click on the **Tracking number groups** menu item within the **Dimensions** folder of the **Setup** group.

Step 2: Open the Tracking number groups form through the menu search

Another way that we can find the **Tracking number groups** form is through the menu search feature.

We can do this by clicking on the search icon in the header of the form (or by pressing **ALT+G**) and then type in **tracking num** storage into the search box. Then you will be able to select the **Tracking number groups** form from the dropdown list.

This will open up the **Tracking number groups** maintenance form where we will be maintaining all of the different number sequences for our batch and serial numbers.

DYNAMICS COMPANIONS
BARE BONES CONFIGURATION GUIDE

CONFIGURING INVENTORY MANAGEMENT WITHIN DYNAMICS 365 FOR FINANCE & OPERATIONS
MODULE 5: CONFIGURING BATCH AND SERIALIZED PRODUCTS

Opening the Tracking number groups maintenance form

How to do it...

Step 1: Open the Tracking number groups form through the menu

We can get to the **Tracking number groups** form a couple of different ways. The first way is through the master menu.

To do this, open up the navigation panel, expand out the **Modules** and group, and click on **Inventory management** to see all of the menu items that are available. Then click on the **Tracking number groups** menu item within the **Dimensions** folder of the **Setup** group.

dyn c
www.dynamicscompanions.com
Dynamics Companions
- 9 -
www.blindsquirrelpublishing.com
© 2019 Blind Squirrel Publishing, LLC , All Rights Reserved
BLIND SQUIRREL
PUBLISHING

DYNAMICS COMPANIONS
BARE BONES CONFIGURATION GUIDE

CONFIGURING INVENTORY MANAGEMENT WITHIN DYNAMICS 365 FOR FINANCE & OPERATIONS
MODULE 5: CONFIGURING BATCH AND SERIALIZED PRODUCTS

Opening the Tracking number groups maintenance form

How to do it...

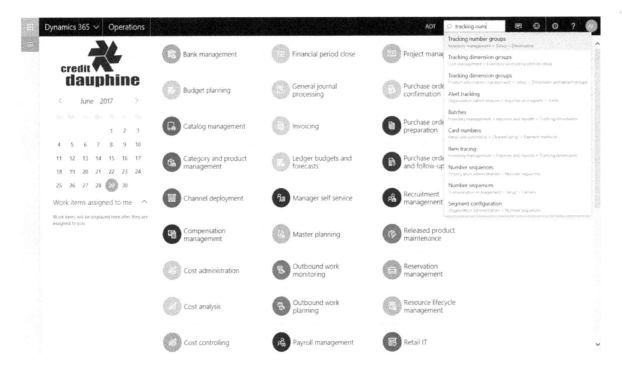

Step 2: Open the Tracking number groups form through the menu search

Another way that we can find the **Tracking number groups** form is through the menu search feature.

We can do this by clicking on the search icon in the header of the form (or by pressing **ALT+G**) and then type in **tracking num** storage into the search box. Then you will be able to select the **Tracking number groups** form from the dropdown list.

dyn c
www.dynamicscompanions.com
Dynamics Companions

- 10 -

www.blindsquirrelpublishing.com
© 2019 Blind Squirrel Publishing, LLC , All Rights Reserved

BLIND SQUIRREL
PUBLISHING

DYNAMICS COMPANIONS
BARE BONES CONFIGURATION GUIDE

CONFIGURING INVENTORY MANAGEMENT WITHIN DYNAMICS 365 FOR FINANCE & OPERATIONS
MODULE 5: CONFIGURING BATCH AND SERIALIZED PRODUCTS

Opening the Tracking number groups maintenance form

How to do it...

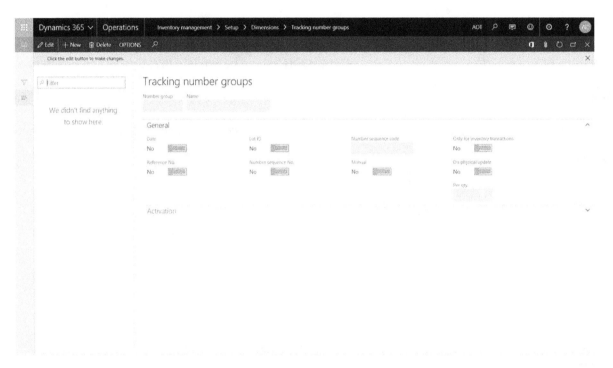

Step 2: Open the Tracking number groups form through the menu search

This will open up the **Tracking number groups** maintenance form where we will be maintaining all of the different number sequences for our batch and serial numbers.

www.dynamicscompanions.com
Dynamics Companions

- 11 -

www.blindsquirrelpublishing.com
© 2019 Blind Squirrel Publishing, LLC, All Rights Reserved

BLIND SQUIRREL
PUBLISHING

DYNAMICS COMPANIONS
BARE BONES CONFIGURATION GUIDE

CONFIGURING INVENTORY MANAGEMENT WITHIN DYNAMICS 365 FOR FINANCE & OPERATIONS
MODULE 5: CONFIGURING BATCH AND SERIALIZED PRODUCTS

Creating a Batch Date Tracking number group

Let's start off by creating a tracking number that incorporates the batch date into the number sequence.

How to do it...

Step 1: Click New

We will start off by adding a new tracking number group record.

To do this just click on the **New** button.

Step 2: Update the Number group

Next we will want to give our tracking number a group code that we can use to quickly reference it.

To do this we will just need to update the **Number group** value.

For this example, we will want to set the **Number group** to **BATCHDATE**.

Step 3: Update the Name

And then we will want to add a more descriptive name for the tracking number group

.

To do this we will just need to update the **Name** value.

For this example, we will want to set the **Name** to **Batch Numbering by Date**.

Step 4: Toggle the Lot ID

For this number sequence we don't want to include the **Lot ID** in the number sequence so we will want to disable that feature.

To do this we will just need to toggle the **Lot ID** option.

For this example, we will want to click on the **Lot ID** toggle switch and set it to the **No** value.

Step 5: Toggle the Number sequence no.

But we do want to have a sequential number included in this tracking group.

To do this we will just need to toggle the **Number sequence no.** option.

For this example, we will want to click on the **Number sequence no.** toggle switch and set it to the **Yes** value.

DYNAMICS COMPANIONS
BARE BONES CONFIGURATION GUIDE

CONFIGURING INVENTORY MANAGEMENT WITHIN DYNAMICS 365 FOR FINANCE & OPERATIONS
MODULE 5: CONFIGURING BATCH AND SERIALIZED PRODUCTS

Creating a Batch Date Tracking number group

How to do it...

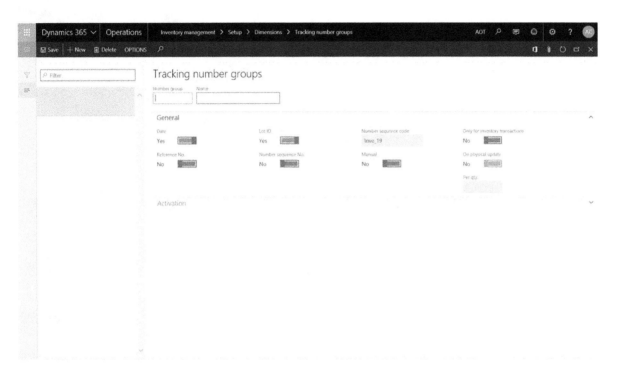

Step 1: Click New

We will start off by adding a new tracking number group record.

To do this just click on the **New** button.

www.dynamicscompanions.com
Dynamics Companions

- 13 -

www.blindsquirrelpublishing.com
© 2019 Blind Squirrel Publishing, LLC, All Rights Reserved

BLIND SQUIRREL
PUBLISHING

DYNAMICS COMPANIONS
BARE BONES CONFIGURATION GUIDE

CONFIGURING INVENTORY MANAGEMENT WITHIN DYNAMICS 365 FOR FINANCE & OPERATIONS
MODULE 5: CONFIGURING BATCH AND SERIALIZED PRODUCTS

Creating a Batch Date Tracking number group

How to do it...

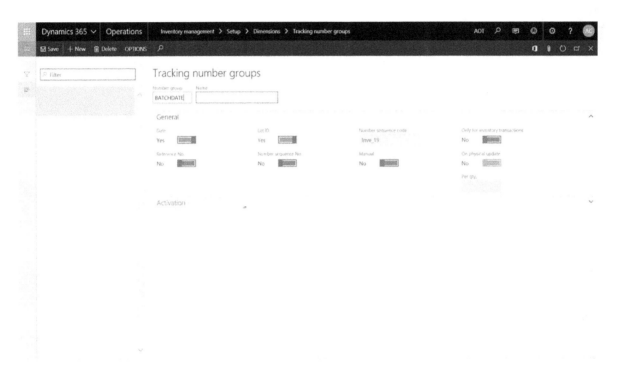

Step 2: Update the Number group

Next we will want to give our tracking number a group code that we can use to quickly reference it.

To do this we will just need to update the **Number group** value.

For this example, we will want to set the **Number group** to **BATCHDATE**.

www.dynamicscompanions.com
Dynamics Companions

- 14 -

www.blindsquirrelpublishing.com
© 2019 Blind Squirrel Publishing, LLC , All Rights Reserved

BLIND SQUIRREL
PUBLISHING

DYNAMICS COMPANIONS
BARE BONES CONFIGURATION GUIDE

CONFIGURING INVENTORY MANAGEMENT WITHIN DYNAMICS 365 FOR FINANCE & OPERATIONS
MODULE 5: CONFIGURING BATCH AND SERIALIZED PRODUCTS

Creating a Batch Date Tracking number group

How to do it...

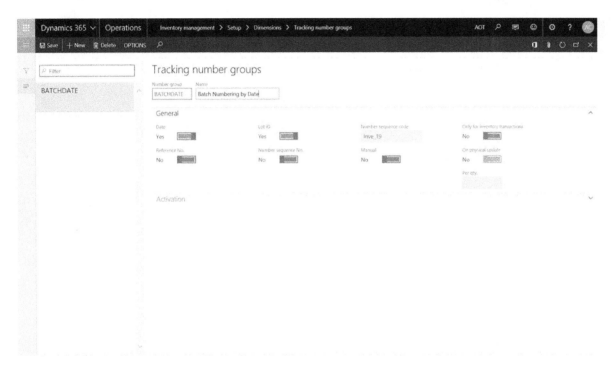

Step 3: Update the Name

And then we will want to add a more descriptive name for the tracking number group .

To do this we will just need to update the **Name** value.

For this example, we will want to set the **Name** to **Batch Numbering by Date**.

dyn c
www.dynamicscompanions.com
Dynamics Companions

- 15 -

www.blindsquirrelpublishing.com
© 2019 Blind Squirrel Publishing, LLC , All Rights Reserved

BLIND SQUIRREL
PUBLISHING

DYNAMICS COMPANIONS
BARE BONES CONFIGURATION GUIDE

CONFIGURING INVENTORY MANAGEMENT WITHIN DYNAMICS 365 FOR FINANCE & OPERATIONS
MODULE 5: CONFIGURING BATCH AND SERIALIZED PRODUCTS

Creating a Batch Date Tracking number group

How to do it...

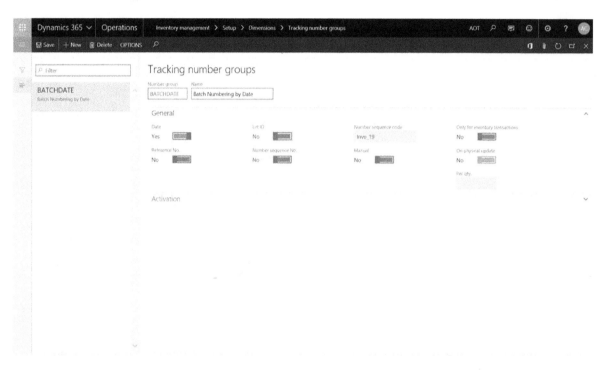

Step 4: Toggle the Lot ID

For this number sequence we don't want to include the **Lot ID** in the number sequence so we will want to disable that feature.

To do this we will just need to toggle the **Lot ID** option.

For this example, we will want to click on the **Lot ID** toggle switch and set it to the **No** value.

www.dynamicscompanions.com
Dynamics Companions

- 16 -

www.blindsquirrelpublishing.com
© 2019 Blind Squirrel Publishing, LLC , All Rights Reserved

BLIND SQUIRREL
PUBLISHING

DYNAMICS COMPANIONS
BARE BONES CONFIGURATION GUIDE

CONFIGURING INVENTORY MANAGEMENT WITHIN DYNAMICS 365 FOR FINANCE & OPERATIONS
MODULE 5: CONFIGURING BATCH AND SERIALIZED PRODUCTS

Creating a Batch Date Tracking number group

How to do it...

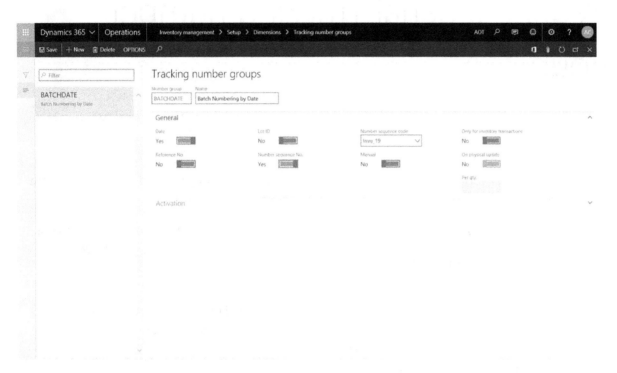

Step 5: Toggle the Number sequence no.

But we do want to have a sequential number included in this tracking group.

To do this we will just need to toggle the **Number sequence no.** option.

For this example, we will want to click on the **Number sequence no.** toggle switch and set it to the **Yes** value.

dync
www.dynamicscompanions.com
Dynamics Companions

- 17 -

www.blindsquirrelpublishing.com
© 2019 Blind Squirrel Publishing, LLC , All Rights Reserved

BLIND SQUIRREL
PUBLISHING

DYNAMICS COMPANIONS
BARE BONES CONFIGURATION GUIDE

CONFIGURING INVENTORY MANAGEMENT WITHIN DYNAMICS 365 FOR FINANCE & OPERATIONS
MODULE 5: CONFIGURING BATCH AND SERIALIZED PRODUCTS

Creating a Serial Tracking number group

Next we will want to create a tracking number group to track serial numbers on products.

How to do it...

Step 1: Click New

We will want to add a new tracking number group record.

To do this just click on the **New** button.

Step 2: Update the Number group

Next we will add a code that we can use to identify the serial tracking group.

To do this we will just need to update the **Number group** value.

For this example, we will want to set the **Number group** to **SERIAL**.

Step 3: Update the Name

And then add a more detailed description of the code.

To do this we will just need to update the **Name** value.

For this example, we will want to set the **Name** to **Serial Numbering**.

Step 4: Toggle the Date

For the serial numbers we will not want to include the date in the tracking code which is selected by default.

To do this we will just need to toggle the **Date** option.

For this example, we will want to click on the **Date** toggle switch and set it to the **No** value.

Step 5: Toggle the Lot ID

Also, we will not want to include a lot number in the serial tracking group either.

To do this we will just need to toggle the **Lot ID** option.

For this example, we will want to click on the **Lot ID** toggle switch and set it to the **No** value.

Step 6: Toggle the Number sequence no.

We do however want to have a sequential number used for our serial numbers.

To do this we will just need to toggle the **Number sequence no.** option.

For this example, we will want to click on the **Number sequence no.** toggle switch and set it to the **Yes** value.

Step 7: Toggle the Only for inventory transactions

And also we will want to mark this number group that it may only be used for inventory transactions

DYNAMICS COMPANIONS
BARE BONES CONFIGURATION GUIDE

CONFIGURING INVENTORY MANAGEMENT WITHIN DYNAMICS 365 FOR FINANCE & OPERATIONS
MODULE 5: CONFIGURING BATCH AND SERIALIZED PRODUCTS

To do this we will just need to toggle the **Only for inventory transactions** option.

For this example, we will want to click on the **Only for inventory transactions** toggle switch and set it to the **Yes** value.

Step 8: Toggle the On physical update

And also we only want this sequence code to be used on the update of inventory.

To do this we will just need to toggle the **On physical update** option.

For this example, we will want to click on the **On physical update** toggle switch and set it to the **Yes** value.

Step 9: Update the Per qty

Finally we will want to tell the system how may units will be included in each serial number. We will want to have a unique serial number for each unit in this case.

To do this we will just need to update the **Per qty** value.

For this example, we will want to set the **Per qty** to **1**.

 www.dynamicscompanions.com
Dynamics Companions

www.blindsquirrelpublishing.com
© 2019 Blind Squirrel Publishing, LLC , All Rights Reserved

BLIND SQUIRREL
PUBLISHING

DYNAMICS COMPANIONS
BARE BONES CONFIGURATION GUIDE

CONFIGURING INVENTORY MANAGEMENT WITHIN DYNAMICS 365 FOR FINANCE & OPERATIONS
MODULE 5: CONFIGURING BATCH AND SERIALIZED PRODUCTS

Creating a Serial Tracking number group

How to do it...

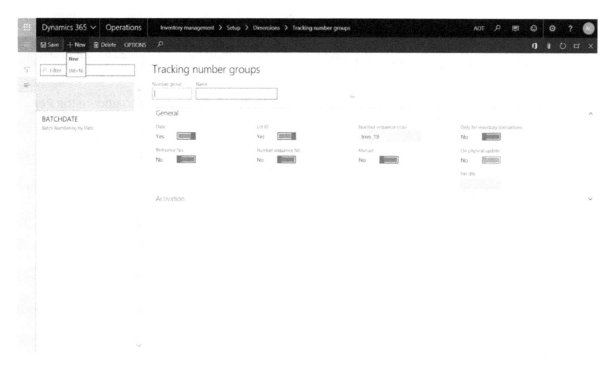

Step 1: Click New

We will want to add a new tracking number group record.

To do this just click on the **New** button.

dync
www.dynamicscompanions.com
Dynamics Companions

- 20 -

www.blindsquirrelpublishing.com
© 2019 Blind Squirrel Publishing, LLC , All Rights Reserved

BLIND SQUIRREL
PUBLISHING

DYNAMICS COMPANIONS
BARE BONES CONFIGURATION GUIDE

CONFIGURING INVENTORY MANAGEMENT WITHIN DYNAMICS 365 FOR FINANCE & OPERATIONS
MODULE 5: CONFIGURING BATCH AND SERIALIZED PRODUCTS

Creating a Serial Tracking number group

How to do it...

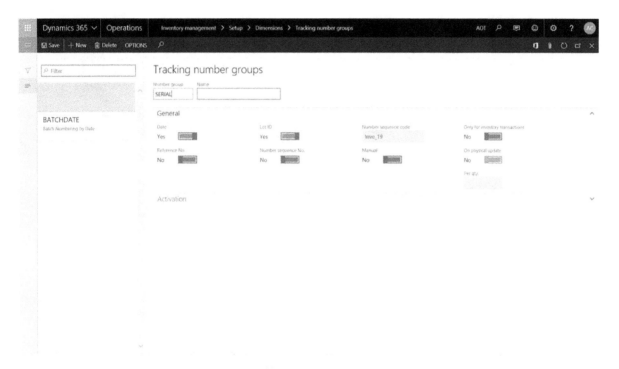

Step 2: Update the Number group

Next we will add a code that we can use to identify the serial tracking group.

To do this we will just need to update the **Number group** value.

For this example, we will want to set the **Number group** to **SERIAL**.

dync
www.dynamicscompanions.com
Dynamics Companions

- 21 -

www.blindsquirrelpublishing.com
© 2019 Blind Squirrel Publishing, LLC, All Rights Reserved

BLIND SQUIRREL
PUBLISHING

DYNAMICS COMPANIONS
BARE BONES CONFIGURATION GUIDE

CONFIGURING INVENTORY MANAGEMENT WITHIN DYNAMICS 365 FOR FINANCE & OPERATIONS
MODULE 5: CONFIGURING BATCH AND SERIALIZED PRODUCTS

Creating a Serial Tracking number group

How to do it...

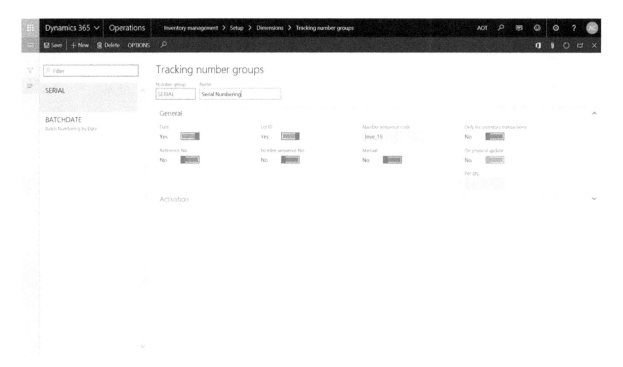

Step 3: Update the Name

And then add a more detailed description of the code.

To do this we will just need to update the **Name** value.

For this example, we will want to set the **Name** to **Serial Numbering**.

dync
www.dynamicscompanions.com
Dynamics Companions

- 22 -

www.blindsquirrelpublishing.com
© 2019 Blind Squirrel Publishing, LLC , All Rights Reserved

BLIND SQUIRREL
PUBLISHING

DYNAMICS COMPANIONS
BARE BONES CONFIGURATION GUIDE

CONFIGURING INVENTORY MANAGEMENT WITHIN DYNAMICS 365 FOR FINANCE & OPERATIONS
MODULE 5: CONFIGURING BATCH AND SERIALIZED PRODUCTS

Creating a Serial Tracking number group

How to do it...

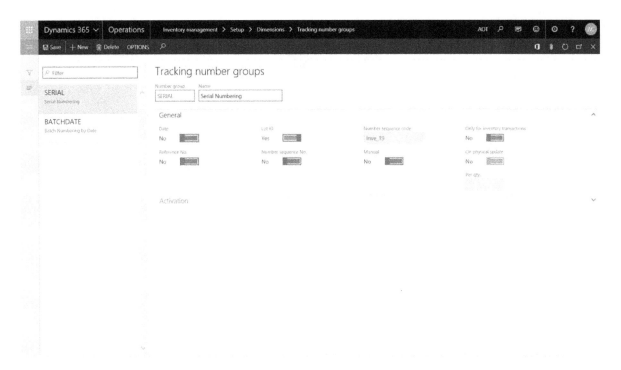

Step 4: Toggle the Date

For the serial numbers we will not want to include the date in the tracking code which is selected by default.

To do this we will just need to toggle the **Date** option.

For this example, we will want to click on the **Date** toggle switch and set it to the **No** value.

www.dynamicscompanions.com
Dynamics Companions

- 23 -

www.blindsquirrelpublishing.com
© 2019 Blind Squirrel Publishing, LLC , All Rights Reserved

BLIND SQUIRREL
PUBLISHING

DYNAMICS COMPANIONS
BARE BONES CONFIGURATION GUIDE

CONFIGURING INVENTORY MANAGEMENT WITHIN DYNAMICS 365 FOR FINANCE & OPERATIONS
MODULE 5: CONFIGURING BATCH AND SERIALIZED PRODUCTS

Creating a Serial Tracking number group

How to do it...

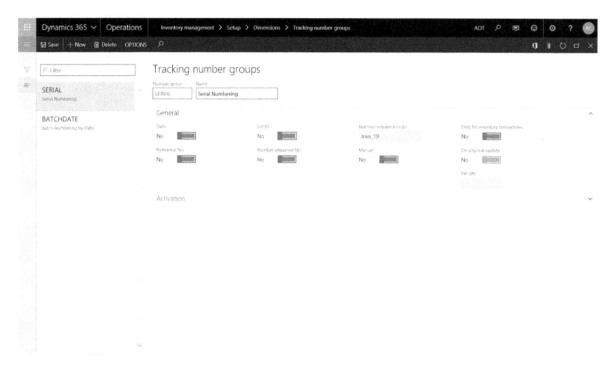

Step 5: Toggle the Lot ID

Also, we will not want to include a lot number in the serial tracking group either.

To do this we will just need to toggle the **Lot ID** option.

For this example, we will want to click on the **Lot ID** toggle switch and set it to the **No** value.

dyn c
www.dynamicscompanions.com
Dynamics Companions

- 24 -

www.blindsquirrelpublishing.com
© 2019 Blind Squirrel Publishing, LLC , All Rights Reserved

BLIND SQUIRREL
PUBLISHING

DYNAMICS COMPANIONS
BARE BONES CONFIGURATION GUIDE

CONFIGURING INVENTORY MANAGEMENT WITHIN DYNAMICS 365 FOR FINANCE & OPERATIONS
MODULE 5: CONFIGURING BATCH AND SERIALIZED PRODUCTS

Creating a Serial Tracking number group

How to do it...

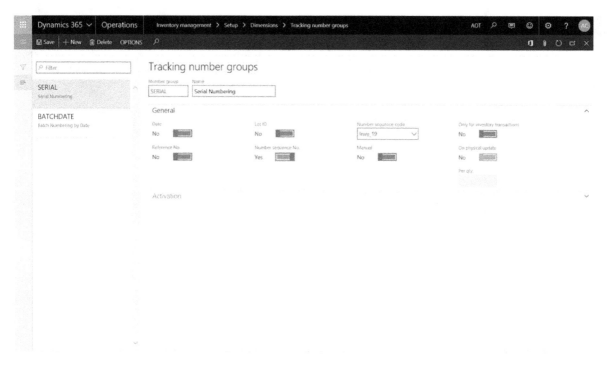

Step 6: Toggle the Number sequence no.

We do however want to have a sequential number used for our serial numbers.

To do this we will just need to toggle the **Number sequence no.** option.

For this example, we will want to click on the **Number sequence no.** toggle switch and set it to the **Yes** value.

www.dynamicscompanions.com
Dynamics Companions

- 25 -

www.blindsquirrelpublishing.com
© 2019 Blind Squirrel Publishing, LLC, All Rights Reserved

BLIND SQUIRREL
PUBLISHING

DYNAMICS COMPANIONS
BARE BONES CONFIGURATION GUIDE

CONFIGURING INVENTORY MANAGEMENT WITHIN DYNAMICS 365 FOR FINANCE & OPERATIONS
MODULE 5: CONFIGURING BATCH AND SERIALIZED PRODUCTS

Creating a Serial Tracking number group

How to do it...

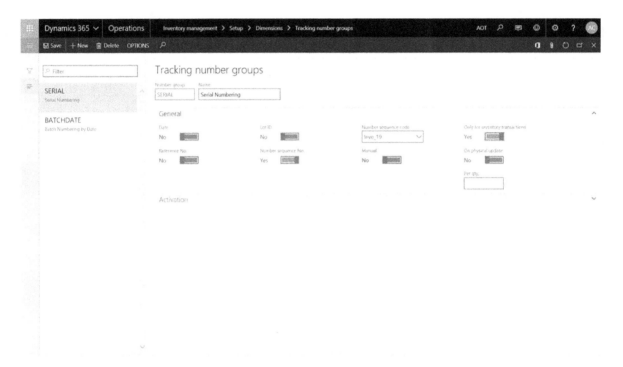

Step 7: Toggle the Only for inventory transactions

And also we will want to mark this number group that it may only be used for inventory transactions

To do this we will just need to toggle the **Only for inventory transactions** option.

For this example, we will want to click on the **Only for inventory transactions** toggle switch and set it to the **Yes** value.

www.dynamicscompanions.com
Dynamics Companions

- 26 -

www.blindsquirrelpublishing.com
© 2019 Blind Squirrel Publishing, LLC, All Rights Reserved

BLIND SQUIRREL
PUBLISHING

DYNAMICS COMPANIONS
BARE BONES CONFIGURATION GUIDE

CONFIGURING INVENTORY MANAGEMENT WITHIN DYNAMICS 365 FOR FINANCE & OPERATIONS
MODULE 5: CONFIGURING BATCH AND SERIALIZED PRODUCTS

Creating a Serial Tracking number group

How to do it...

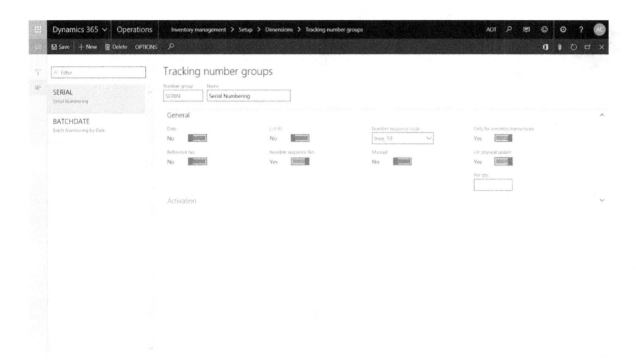

Step 8: Toggle the On physical update

And also we only want this sequence code to be used on the update of inventory.

To do this we will just need to toggle the **On physical update** option.

For this example, we will want to click on the **On physical update** toggle switch and set it to the **Yes** value.

www.dynamicscompanions.com
Dynamics Companions

- 27 -

www.blindsquirrelpublishing.com
© 2019 Blind Squirrel Publishing, LLC , All Rights Reserved

BLIND SQUIRREL
PUBLISHING

DYNAMICS COMPANIONS
BARE BONES CONFIGURATION GUIDE

CONFIGURING INVENTORY MANAGEMENT WITHIN DYNAMICS 365 FOR FINANCE & OPERATIONS
MODULE 5: CONFIGURING BATCH AND SERIALIZED PRODUCTS

Creating a Serial Tracking number group

How to do it...

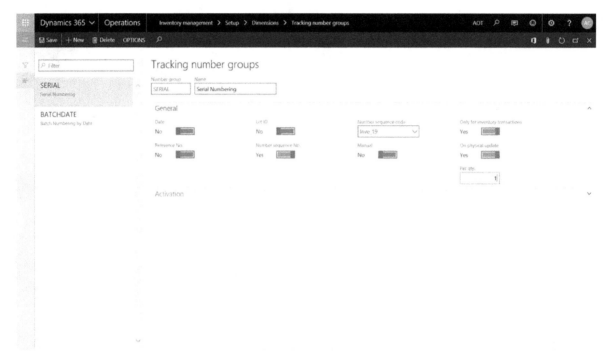

Step 9: Update the Per qty

Finally we will want to tell the system how may units will be included in each serial number. We will want to have a unique serial number for each unit in this case.

To do this we will just need to update the **Per qty** value.

For this example, we will want to set the **Per qty** to **1**.

www.dynamicscompanions.com
Dynamics Companions

- 28 -

www.blindsquirrelpublishing.com
© 2019 Blind Squirrel Publishing, LLC , All Rights Reserved

BLIND SQUIRREL
PUBLISHING

DYNAMICS COMPANIONS
BARE BONES CONFIGURATION GUIDE

CONFIGURING INVENTORY MANAGEMENT WITHIN DYNAMICS 365 FOR FINANCE & OPERATIONS
MODULE 5: CONFIGURING BATCH AND SERIALIZED PRODUCTS

Creating a Serial Tracking number group

Review

Now we have created all of the tracking number groups that we need to start tracking batch and serialized products.

DYNAMICS COMPANIONS
BARE BONES CONFIGURATION GUIDE

CONFIGURING INVENTORY MANAGEMENT WITHIN DYNAMICS 365 FOR FINANCE & OPERATIONS
MODULE 5: CONFIGURING BATCH AND SERIALIZED PRODUCTS

Configuring A Batch Controlled Product

Now that we have a numbering group that will create our batch numbers for us, we can start using it on a product to have the system assign new batch numbers as the products are received in.

Topics Covered

- Creating a Batch Controlled Product

- Creating Batch Tracked Inventory

- Viewing Batch Details

www.dynamicscompanions.com
Dynamics Companions

- 30 -

www.blindsquirrelpublishing.com
© 2019 Blind Squirrel Publishing, LLC , All Rights Reserved

BLIND SQUIRREL
PUBLISHING

DYNAMICS COMPANIONS
BARE BONES CONFIGURATION GUIDE

CONFIGURING INVENTORY MANAGEMENT WITHIN DYNAMICS 365 FOR FINANCE & OPERATIONS
MODULE 5: CONFIGURING BATCH AND SERIALIZED PRODUCTS

Creating a Batch Controlled Product

Since all of the products that we have created so far are traditional products and not tracked as batches we will want to start off by creating a new released product that is batch controlled.

How to do it...

Step 1: Click New

Now we will want to return back to the Released Products maintenance form and create a new product which we will add tracking dimensions to.

To do this just click on the **New** button.

This will open up the **New released product** dialog form where we will start to configure our new product.

Step 2: Update the Product number

We will start off by giving our product a product number to identify it.

To do this we will just need to update the **Product number** value.

For this example, we will want to set the **Product number** to **00569651**.

Step 3: Update the Product name

And then we will give our new product a more descriptive name.

To do this we will just need to update the **Product name** value.

For this example, we will want to set the **Product name** to **8KV Cable 3C-4/0 High Voltage**.

Step 4: Select the Item model group

We will want to assign our product to an item model group.

To do this we will just need to select the **Item model group** from the dropdown list.

For this example, we will want to click on the **Item model group** dropdown list and select **STD**.

Step 5: Select the Item group

And also assign an item group to the new product.

To do this we will just need to select the **Item group** from the dropdown list.

For this example, we will want to click on the **Item group** dropdown list and select **DEFAULT**.

Step 6: Select the Storage dimension group

We will want to track this product down to the inventory location which we will to by setting the storage dimension for the new product.

DYNAMICS COMPANIONS
BARE BONES CONFIGURATION GUIDE

CONFIGURING INVENTORY MANAGEMENT WITHIN DYNAMICS 365 FOR FINANCE & OPERATIONS
MODULE 5: CONFIGURING BATCH AND SERIALIZED PRODUCTS

To do this we will just need to select the **Storage dimension group** from the dropdown list.

For this example, we will want to click on the **Storage dimension group** dropdown list and select **LOC**.

Step 7: Select the Tracking dimension group

And we will also want to indicate that we are going to track this product at the batch level through the **Tracking dimension group**.

To do this we will just need to select the **Tracking dimension group** from the dropdown list.

For this example, we will want to click on the **Tracking dimension group** dropdown list and select **BATCH**.

Step 8: Select the Inventory unit

Now we will need to identify the units of measure that we will be tracking the inventory at.

To do this we will just need to select the **Inventory unit** from the dropdown list.

For this example, we will want to click on the **Inventory unit** dropdown list and select **ft**.

Step 9: Select the Purchase unit

We will want to set a unit of measure that we will use when purchasing the product.

To do this we will just need to select the **Purchase unit** from the dropdown list.

For this example, we will want to click on the **Purchase unit** dropdown list and select **ft**.

Step 10: Select the Sales unit

We will assign the product a default unit of measure for all sales transactions.

To do this we will just need to select the **Sales unit** from the dropdown list.

For this example, we will want to click on the **Sales unit** dropdown list and select **ft**.

Step 11: Select the BOM unit

And we will set the default unit of measure for all production and bills of material.

To do this we will just need to select the **BOM unit** from the dropdown list.

For this example, we will want to click on the **BOM unit** dropdown list and select **ft**.

Step 12: Click OK

Now that we have finished assigning all of the default details for the product we can create the released product.

To do this just click on the **OK** button.

That will take us to the larger maintenance form for our product. Now we will want to add some finishing touches to the product configuration.

Step 13: Select the Calculation group

We will want to assign a **Calculation group** to our new product which we will find in the **Engineer** tab group.

To do this we will just need to select the **Calculation group** from the dropdown list.

For this example, we will want to click on the **Calculation group** dropdown list and select **DEFAULT**.

Step 14: Update the Purchase Price

We will also want to set the purchase price for the product which we will see in the **Purchase** tab group.

To do this we will just need to update the **Purchase Price** value.

www.dynamicscompanions.com
Dynamics Companions

- 32 -

www.blindsquirrelpublishing.com
© 2019 Blind Squirrel Publishing, LLC , All Rights Reserved

BLIND SQUIRREL
PUBLISHING

DYNAMICS COMPANIONS
BARE BONES CONFIGURATION GUIDE

CONFIGURING INVENTORY MANAGEMENT WITHIN DYNAMICS 365 FOR FINANCE & OPERATIONS
MODULE 5: CONFIGURING BATCH AND SERIALIZED PRODUCTS

For this example, we will want to set the **Purchase Price** to **9.87**.

Step 15: Click Item price

Now that we have set the purchase price for the product we well want to do a cost rollup to create a standard cost record for the product.

To do this just click on the **Item price** button.

Step 16: Click Calculate item cost

When the **Item price** form is displayed we will want to perform a cost calculation.

To do this just click on the **Calculate item cost** button.

This will open up the calculation parameters dialog panel.

Step 17: Select the Costing group, select the Site and click OK

Now we will want to specify the costing version that we want to calculate the cost for and also the site that we want the cost to apply to.

To do this we will just need to select the **Costing group** from the dropdown list, select the **Site** from the dropdown list and click on the **OK** button.

For this example, we will want to click on the **Costing group** dropdown list and select **STD**, click on the **Site** dropdown list and select **SD12**.

Step 18: Click Activate pending price(s)

When we return back to the **Item price** form we will see that there is now a pending cost that is associated with the product. All we need to do now is to activate the product price.

To do this just click on the **Activate pending price(s)** button.

After we have done that we will be able to see that the price has now been activated for us and will be used by the system for all inventory costing journals. We can now exit from the form.

Step 19: Expand Manage inventory fast tab

Next we will need to define some of the default inventory management settings for the product.

To do this we will want to return to the product that you just created and expand out the **Manage Inventory** tab group.

Step 20: Select the Batch number group

Since this product is tracked in batches we will want to assign a tracking number code to the **Batch number group** for the product.

To do this we will just need to select the **Batch number group** from the dropdown list.

For this example, we will want to click on the **Batch number group** dropdown list and select **BATCHDATE**.

www.dynamicscompanions.com
Dynamics Companions

- 33 -

www.blindsquirrelpublishing.com
© 2019 Blind Squirrel Publishing, LLC, All Rights Reserved

BLIND SQUIRREL
PUBLISHING

DYNAMICS COMPANIONS
BARE BONES CONFIGURATION GUIDE

CONFIGURING INVENTORY MANAGEMENT WITHIN DYNAMICS 365 FOR FINANCE & OPERATIONS
MODULE 5: CONFIGURING BATCH AND SERIALIZED PRODUCTS

Creating a Batch Controlled Product

How to do it...

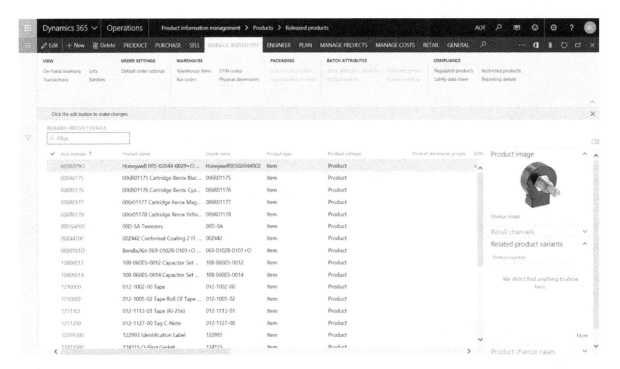

Step 1: Click New

Now we will want to return back to the Released Products maintenance form and create a new product which we will add tracking dimensions to.

To do this just click on the **New** button.

www.dynamicscompanions.com
Dynamics Companions

- 34 -

www.blindsquirrelpublishing.com
© 2019 Blind Squirrel Publishing, LLC , All Rights Reserved

BLIND SQUIRREL
PUBLISHING

DYNAMICS COMPANIONS
BARE BONES CONFIGURATION GUIDE

CONFIGURING INVENTORY MANAGEMENT WITHIN DYNAMICS 365 FOR FINANCE & OPERATIONS
MODULE 5: CONFIGURING BATCH AND SERIALIZED PRODUCTS

Creating a Batch Controlled Product

How to do it...

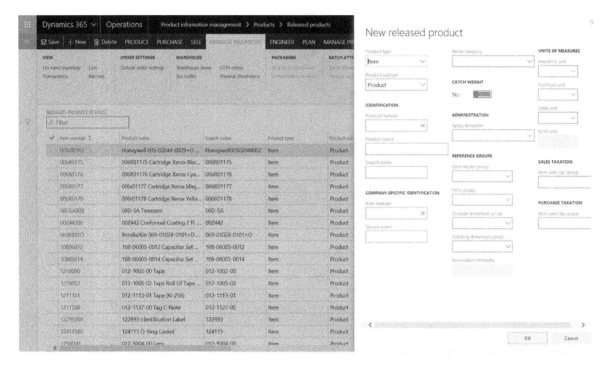

Step 1: Click New

This will open up the **New released product** dialog form where we will start to configure our new product.

www.dynamicscompanions.com
Dynamics Companions

- 35 -

www.blindsquirrelpublishing.com
© 2019 Blind Squirrel Publishing, LLC , All Rights Reserved

BLIND SQUIRREL
PUBLISHING

DYNAMICS COMPANIONS
BARE BONES CONFIGURATION GUIDE

CONFIGURING INVENTORY MANAGEMENT WITHIN DYNAMICS 365 FOR FINANCE & OPERATIONS
MODULE 5: CONFIGURING BATCH AND SERIALIZED PRODUCTS

Creating a Batch Controlled Product

How to do it...

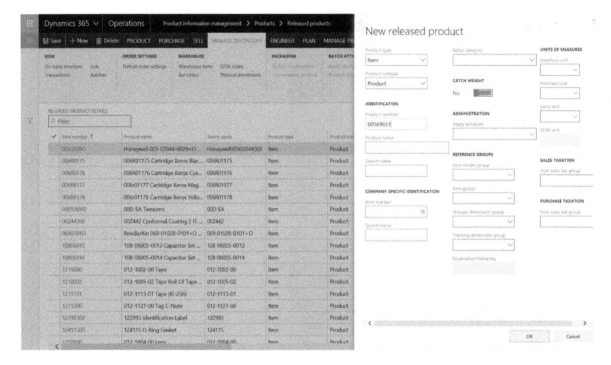

Step 2: Update the Product number

We will start off by giving our product a product number to identify it.

To do this we will just need to update the **Product number** value.

For this example, we will want to set the **Product number** to **00569651**.

dyn c
www.dynamicscompanions.com
Dynamics Companions

- 36 -

www.blindsquirrelpublishing.com
© 2019 Blind Squirrel Publishing, LLC , All Rights Reserved

BLIND SQUIRREL
PUBLISHING

DYNAMICS COMPANIONS
BARE BONES CONFIGURATION GUIDE

CONFIGURING INVENTORY MANAGEMENT WITHIN DYNAMICS 365 FOR FINANCE & OPERATIONS
MODULE 5: CONFIGURING BATCH AND SERIALIZED PRODUCTS

Creating a Batch Controlled Product

How to do it...

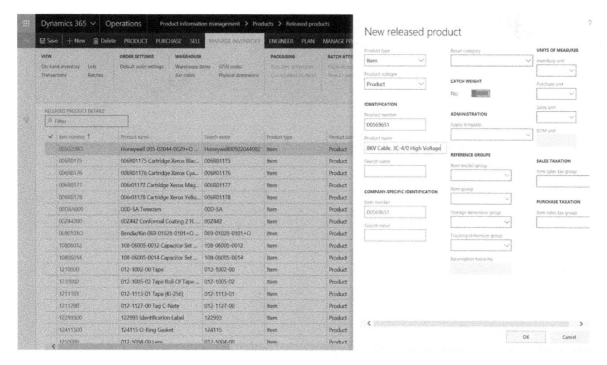

Step 3: Update the Product name

And then we will give our new product a more descriptive name.

To do this we will just need to update the **Product name** value.

For this example, we will want to set the **Product name** to **8KV Cable 3C-4/0 High Voltage**.

dynC
www.dynamicscompanions.com
Dynamics Companions

- 37 -

www.blindsquirrelpublishing.com
© 2019 Blind Squirrel Publishing, LLC , All Rights Reserved

BLIND SQUIRREL
PUBLISHING

DYNAMICS COMPANIONS
BARE BONES CONFIGURATION GUIDE

CONFIGURING INVENTORY MANAGEMENT WITHIN DYNAMICS 365 FOR FINANCE & OPERATIONS
MODULE 5: CONFIGURING BATCH AND SERIALIZED PRODUCTS

Creating a Batch Controlled Product

How to do it...

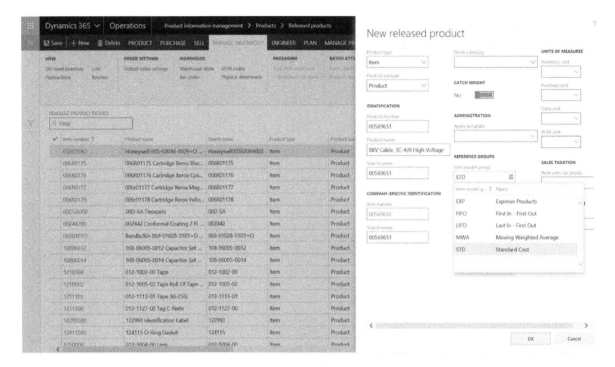

Step 4: Select the Item model group

We will want to assign our product to an item model group.

To do this we will just need to select the **Item model group** from the dropdown list.

For this example, we will want to click on the **Item model group** dropdown list and select **STD**.

dyn c

www.dynamicscompanions.com
Dynamics Companions

- 38 -

www.blindsquirrelpublishing.com
© 2019 Blind Squirrel Publishing, LLC , All Rights Reserved

BLIND SQUIRREL
PUBLISHING

DYNAMICS COMPANIONS
BARE BONES CONFIGURATION GUIDE

CONFIGURING INVENTORY MANAGEMENT WITHIN DYNAMICS 365 FOR FINANCE & OPERATIONS
MODULE 5: CONFIGURING BATCH AND SERIALIZED PRODUCTS

Creating a Batch Controlled Product

How to do it...

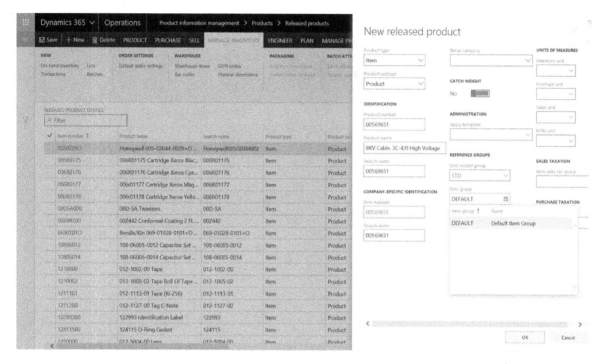

Step 5: Select the Item group

And also assign an item group to the new product.

To do this we will just need to select the **Item group** from the dropdown list.

For this example, we will want to click on the **Item group** dropdown list and select **DEFAULT**.

dyn

www.dynamicscompanions.com
Dynamics Companions

- 39 -

www.blindsquirrelpublishing.com
© 2019 Blind Squirrel Publishing, LLC , All Rights Reserved

BLIND SQUIRREL
PUBLISHING

DYNAMICS COMPANIONS
BARE BONES CONFIGURATION GUIDE

CONFIGURING INVENTORY MANAGEMENT WITHIN DYNAMICS 365 FOR FINANCE & OPERATIONS
MODULE 5: CONFIGURING BATCH AND SERIALIZED PRODUCTS

Creating a Batch Controlled Product

How to do it...

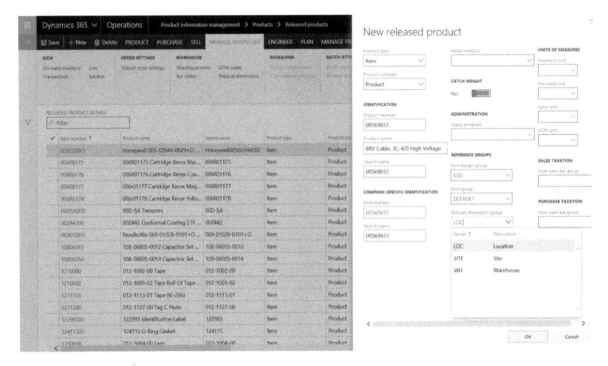

Step 6: Select the Storage dimension group

We will want to track this product down to the inventory location which we will to by setting the storage dimension for the new product.

To do this we will just need to select the **Storage dimension group** from the dropdown list.

For this example, we will want to click on the **Storage dimension group** dropdown list and select **LOC**.

www.dynamicscompanions.com
Dynamics Companions

- 40 -

www.blindsquirrelpublishing.com
© 2019 Blind Squirrel Publishing, LLC , All Rights Reserved

BLIND SQUIRREL
PUBLISHING

DYNAMICS COMPANIONS
BARE BONES CONFIGURATION GUIDE

CONFIGURING INVENTORY MANAGEMENT WITHIN DYNAMICS 365 FOR FINANCE & OPERATIONS
MODULE 5: CONFIGURING BATCH AND SERIALIZED PRODUCTS

Creating a Batch Controlled Product

How to do it...

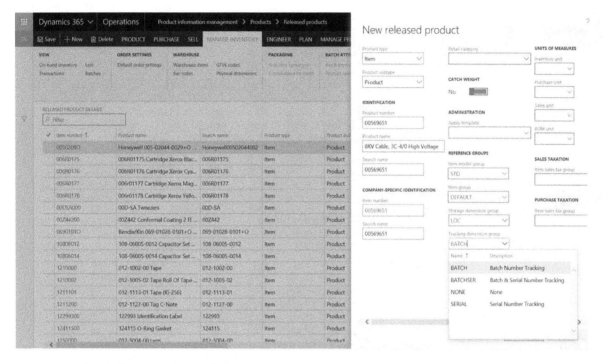

Step 7: Select the Tracking dimension group

And we will also want to indicate that we are going to track this product at the batch level through the **Tracking dimension group**.

To do this we will just need to select the **Tracking dimension group** from the dropdown list.

For this example, we will want to click on the **Tracking dimension group** dropdown list and select **BATCH**.

dync
www.dynamicscompanions.com
Dynamics Companions

- 41 -

www.blindsquirrelpublishing.com
© 2019 Blind Squirrel Publishing, LLC , All Rights Reserved

BLIND SQUIRREL
PUBLISHING

DYNAMICS COMPANIONS
BARE BONES CONFIGURATION GUIDE

CONFIGURING INVENTORY MANAGEMENT WITHIN DYNAMICS 365 FOR FINANCE & OPERATIONS
MODULE 5: CONFIGURING BATCH AND SERIALIZED PRODUCTS

Creating a Batch Controlled Product

How to do it...

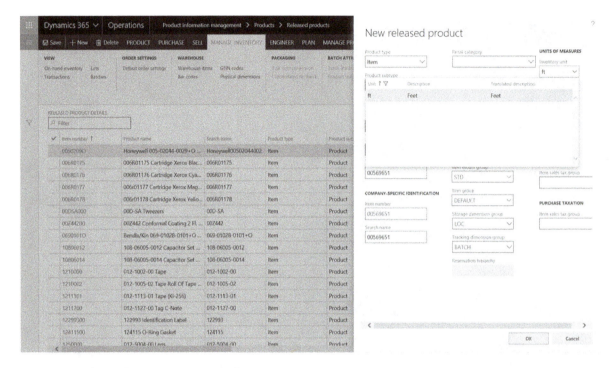

Step 8: Select the Inventory unit

Now we will need to identify the units of measure that we will be tracking the inventory at.

To do this we will just need to select the **Inventory unit** from the dropdown list.

For this example, we will want to click on the **Inventory unit** dropdown list and select **ft**.

dyn c
www.dynamicscompanions.com
Dynamics Companions

- 42 -

www.blindsquirrelpublishing.com
© 2019 Blind Squirrel Publishing, LLC , All Rights Reserved

BLIND SQUIRREL
PUBLISHING

DYNAMICS COMPANIONS
BARE BONES CONFIGURATION GUIDE

CONFIGURING INVENTORY MANAGEMENT WITHIN DYNAMICS 365 FOR FINANCE & OPERATIONS
MODULE 5: CONFIGURING BATCH AND SERIALIZED PRODUCTS

Creating a Batch Controlled Product

How to do it...

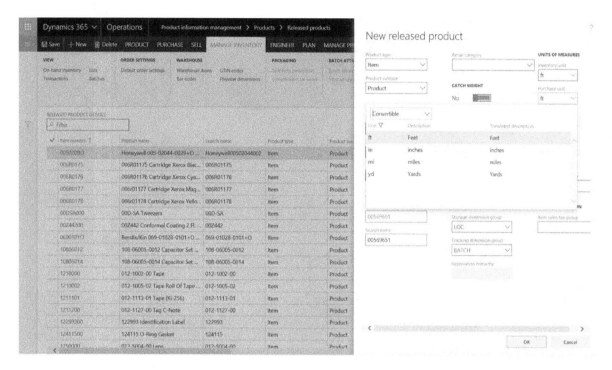

Step 9: Select the Purchase unit

We will want to set a unit of measure that we will use when purchasing the product.

To do this we will just need to select the **Purchase unit** from the dropdown list.

For this example, we will want to click on the **Purchase unit** dropdown list and select **ft**.

www.dynamicscompanions.com
Dynamics Companions

- 43 -

www.blindsquirrelpublishing.com
© 2019 Blind Squirrel Publishing, LLC, All Rights Reserved

BLIND SQUIRREL
PUBLISHING

DYNAMICS COMPANIONS
BARE BONES CONFIGURATION GUIDE

CONFIGURING INVENTORY MANAGEMENT WITHIN DYNAMICS 365 FOR FINANCE & OPERATIONS
MODULE 5: CONFIGURING BATCH AND SERIALIZED PRODUCTS

Creating a Batch Controlled Product

How to do it...

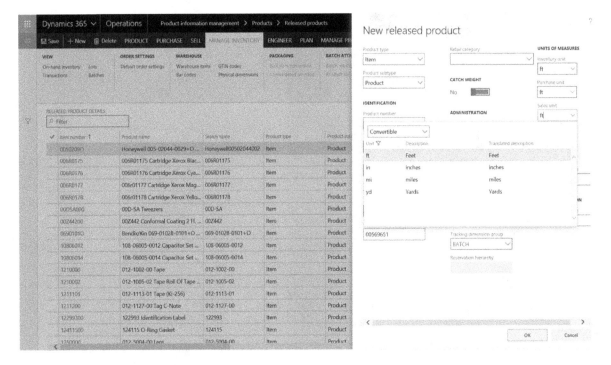

Step 10: Select the Sales unit

We will assign the product a default unit of measure for all sales transactions.

To do this we will just need to select the **Sales unit** from the dropdown list.

For this example, we will want to click on the **Sales unit** dropdown list and select **ft**.

www.dynamicscompanions.com
Dynamics Companions

- 44 -

www.blindsquirrelpublishing.com
© 2019 Blind Squirrel Publishing, LLC , All Rights Reserved

BLIND SQUIRREL
PUBLISHING

DYNAMICS COMPANIONS
BARE BONES CONFIGURATION GUIDE

CONFIGURING INVENTORY MANAGEMENT WITHIN DYNAMICS 365 FOR FINANCE & OPERATIONS
MODULE 5: CONFIGURING BATCH AND SERIALIZED PRODUCTS

Creating a Batch Controlled Product

How to do it...

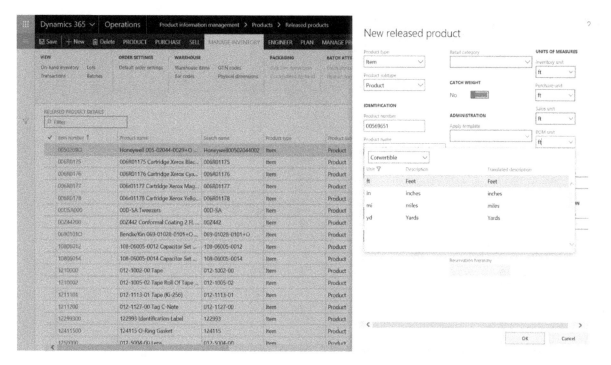

Step 11: Select the BOM unit

And we will set the default unit of measure for all production and bills of material.

To do this we will just need to select the **BOM unit** from the dropdown list.

For this example, we will want to click on the **BOM unit** dropdown list and select **ft**.

www.dynamicscompanions.com
Dynamics Companions

- 45 -

www.blindsquirrelpublishing.com
© 2019 Blind Squirrel Publishing, LLC , All Rights Reserved

BLIND SQUIRREL
PUBLISHING

DYNAMICS COMPANIONS
BARE BONES CONFIGURATION GUIDE

CONFIGURING INVENTORY MANAGEMENT WITHIN DYNAMICS 365 FOR FINANCE & OPERATIONS
MODULE 5: CONFIGURING BATCH AND SERIALIZED PRODUCTS

Creating a Batch Controlled Product

How to do it...

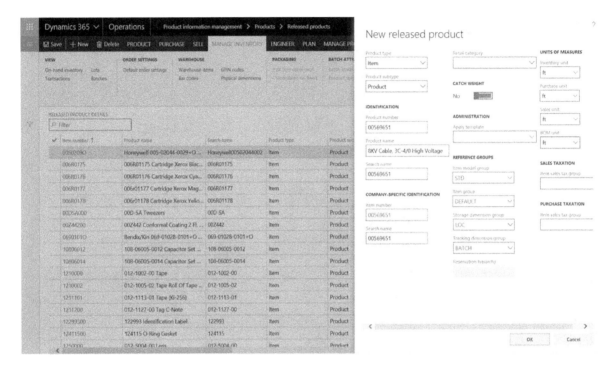

Step 12: Click OK

Now that we have finished assigning all of the default details for the product we can create the released product.

To do this just click on the **OK** button.

dync
www.dynamicscompanions.com
Dynamics Companions

- 46 -

www.blindsquirrelpublishing.com
© 2019 Blind Squirrel Publishing, LLC , All Rights Reserved

BLIND SQUIRREL
PUBLISHING

DYNAMICS COMPANIONS
BARE BONES CONFIGURATION GUIDE

CONFIGURING INVENTORY MANAGEMENT WITHIN DYNAMICS 365 FOR FINANCE & OPERATIONS
MODULE 5: CONFIGURING BATCH AND SERIALIZED PRODUCTS

Creating a Batch Controlled Product

How to do it...

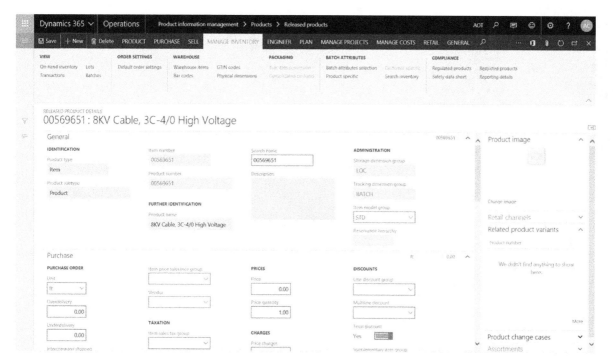

Step 12: Click OK

That will take us to the larger maintenance form for our product. Now we will want to add some finishing touches to the product configuration.

dync
www.dynamicscompanions.com
Dynamics Companions

- 47 -

www.blindsquirrelpublishing.com
© 2019 Blind Squirrel Publishing, LLC, All Rights Reserved

BLIND SQUIRREL
PUBLISHING

DYNAMICS COMPANIONS
BARE BONES CONFIGURATION GUIDE

CONFIGURING INVENTORY MANAGEMENT WITHIN DYNAMICS 365 FOR FINANCE & OPERATIONS
MODULE 5: CONFIGURING BATCH AND SERIALIZED PRODUCTS

Creating a Batch Controlled Product

How to do it...

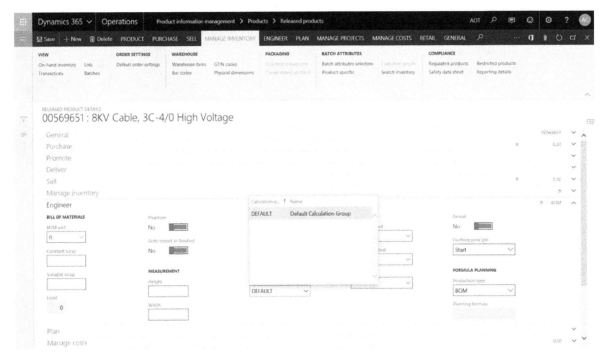

Step 13: Select the Calculation group

We will want to assign a **Calculation group** to our new product which we will find in the **Engineer** tab group.

To do this we will just need to select the **Calculation group** from the dropdown list.

For this example, we will want to click on the **Calculation group** dropdown list and select **DEFAULT**.

www.dynamicscompanions.com
Dynamics Companions

- 48 -

www.blindsquirrelpublishing.com
© 2019 Blind Squirrel Publishing, LLC , All Rights Reserved

BLIND SQUIRREL
PUBLISHING

DYNAMICS COMPANIONS
BARE BONES CONFIGURATION GUIDE

CONFIGURING INVENTORY MANAGEMENT WITHIN DYNAMICS 365 FOR FINANCE & OPERATIONS
MODULE 5: CONFIGURING BATCH AND SERIALIZED PRODUCTS

Creating a Batch Controlled Product

How to do it...

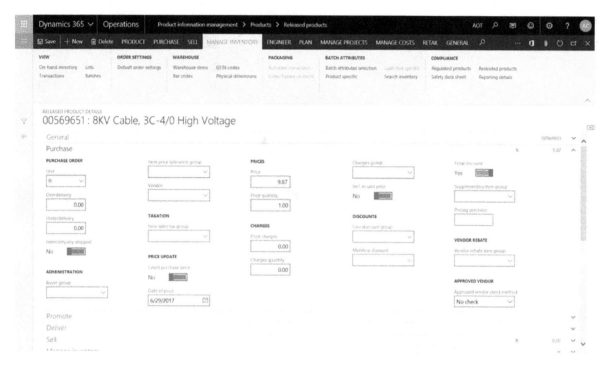

Step 14: Update the Purchase Price

We will also want to set the purchase price for the product which we will see in the **Purchase** tab group.

To do this we will just need to update the **Purchase Price** value.

For this example, we will want to set the **Purchase Price** to **9.87**.

dync   www.dynamicscompanions.com
Dynamics Companions

- 49 -

www.blindsquirrelpublishing.com
© 2019 Blind Squirrel Publishing, LLC , All Rights Reserved

BLIND SQUIRREL
PUBLISHING

DYNAMICS COMPANIONS
BARE BONES CONFIGURATION GUIDE

CONFIGURING INVENTORY MANAGEMENT WITHIN DYNAMICS 365 FOR FINANCE & OPERATIONS
MODULE 5: CONFIGURING BATCH AND SERIALIZED PRODUCTS

Creating a Batch Controlled Product

How to do it...

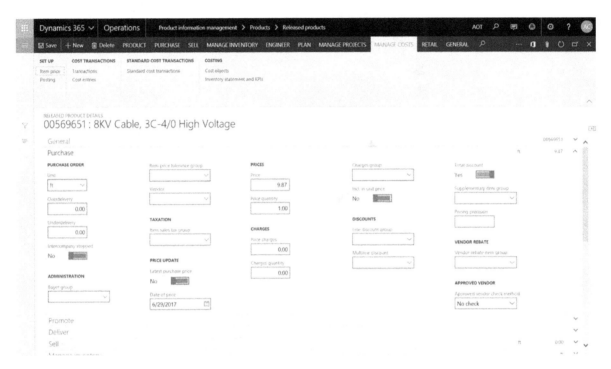

Step 15: Click Item price

Now that we have set the purchase price for the product we well want to do a cost rollup to create a standard cost record for the product.

To do this just click on the **Item price** button.

dync
www.dynamicscompanions.com
Dynamics Companions

- 50 -

www.blindsquirrelpublishing.com
© 2019 Blind Squirrel Publishing, LLC , All Rights Reserved

BLIND SQUIRREL
PUBLISHING

DYNAMICS COMPANIONS
BARE BONES CONFIGURATION GUIDE

CONFIGURING INVENTORY MANAGEMENT WITHIN DYNAMICS 365 FOR FINANCE & OPERATIONS
MODULE 5: CONFIGURING BATCH AND SERIALIZED PRODUCTS

Creating a Batch Controlled Product

How to do it...

Step 16: Click Calculate item cost

When the **Item price** form is displayed we will want to perform a cost calculation.

To do this just click on the **Calculate item cost** button.

www.dynamicscompanions.com
Dynamics Companions

- 51 -

www.blindsquirrelpublishing.com
© 2019 Blind Squirrel Publishing, LLC , All Rights Reserved

BLIND SQUIRREL
PUBLISHING

DYNAMICS COMPANIONS
BARE BONES CONFIGURATION GUIDE

CONFIGURING INVENTORY MANAGEMENT WITHIN DYNAMICS 365 FOR FINANCE & OPERATIONS
MODULE 5: CONFIGURING BATCH AND SERIALIZED PRODUCTS

Creating a Batch Controlled Product

How to do it...

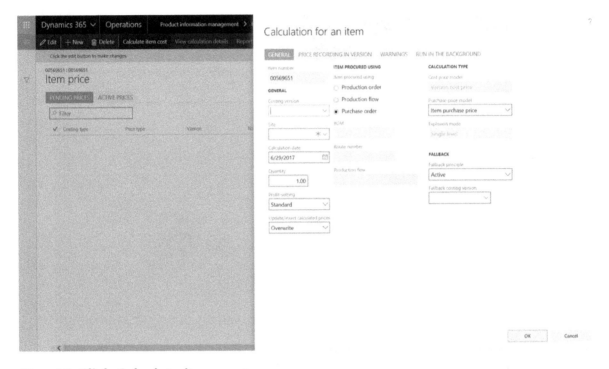

Step 16: Click Calculate item cost

This will open up the calculation parameters dialog panel.

www.dynamicscompanions.com
Dynamics Companions

- 52 -

www.blindsquirrelpublishing.com
© 2019 Blind Squirrel Publishing, LLC , All Rights Reserved

BLIND SQUIRREL
PUBLISHING

DYNAMICS COMPANIONS
BARE BONES CONFIGURATION GUIDE

CONFIGURING INVENTORY MANAGEMENT WITHIN DYNAMICS 365 FOR FINANCE & OPERATIONS
MODULE 5: CONFIGURING BATCH AND SERIALIZED PRODUCTS

Creating a Batch Controlled Product

How to do it...

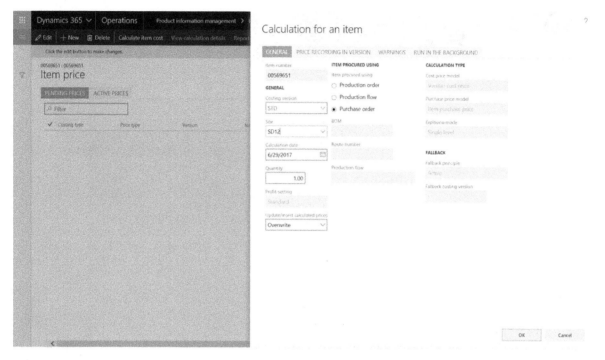

Step 17: Select the Costing group, select the Site and click OK

Now we will want to specify the costing version that we want to calculate the cost for and also the site that we want the cost to apply to.

To do this we will just need to select the **Costing group** from the dropdown list, select the **Site** from the dropdown list and click on the **OK** button.

For this example, we will want to click on the **Costing group** dropdown list and select **STD**, click on the **Site** dropdown list and select **SD12**.

dyn c
www.dynamicscompanions.com
Dynamics Companions

- 53 -

www.blindsquirrelpublishing.com
© 2019 Blind Squirrel Publishing, LLC , All Rights Reserved

BLIND SQUIRREL
PUBLISHING

DYNAMICS COMPANIONS
BARE BONES CONFIGURATION GUIDE

CONFIGURING INVENTORY MANAGEMENT WITHIN DYNAMICS 365 FOR FINANCE & OPERATIONS
MODULE 5: CONFIGURING BATCH AND SERIALIZED PRODUCTS

Creating a Batch Controlled Product

How to do it...

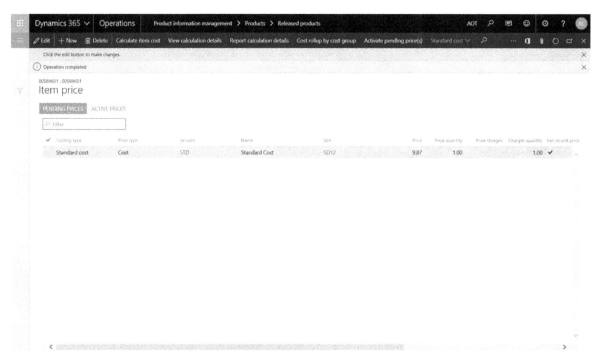

Step 18: Click Activate pending price(s)

When we return back to the **Item price** form we will see that there is now a pending cost that is associated with the product. All we need to do now is to activate the product price.

To do this just click on the **Activate pending price(s)** button.

dyn c
www.dynamicscompanions.com
Dynamics Companions

- 54 -

www.blindsquirrelpublishing.com
© 2019 Blind Squirrel Publishing, LLC , All Rights Reserved

BLIND SQUIRREL
PUBLISHING

DYNAMICS COMPANIONS
BARE BONES CONFIGURATION GUIDE

CONFIGURING INVENTORY MANAGEMENT WITHIN DYNAMICS 365 FOR FINANCE & OPERATIONS
MODULE 5: CONFIGURING BATCH AND SERIALIZED PRODUCTS

Creating a Batch Controlled Product

How to do it...

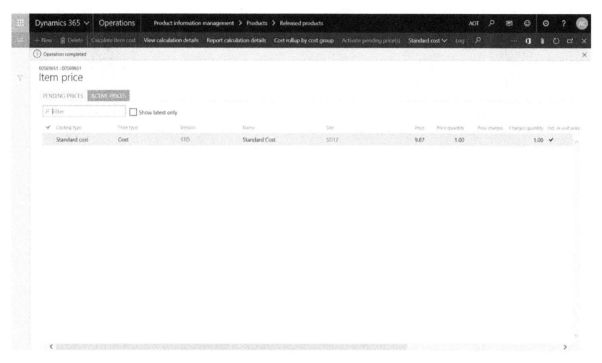

Step 18: Click Activate pending price(s)

After we have done that we will be able to see that the price has now been activated for us and will be used by the system for all inventory costing journals. We can now exit from the form.

www.dynamicscompanions.com
Dynamics Companions

- 55 -

www.blindsquirrelpublishing.com
© 2019 Blind Squirrel Publishing, LLC , All Rights Reserved

BLIND SQUIRREL
PUBLISHING

DYNAMICS COMPANIONS
BARE BONES CONFIGURATION GUIDE

CONFIGURING INVENTORY MANAGEMENT WITHIN DYNAMICS 365 FOR FINANCE & OPERATIONS
MODULE 5: CONFIGURING BATCH AND SERIALIZED PRODUCTS

Creating a Batch Controlled Product

How to do it...

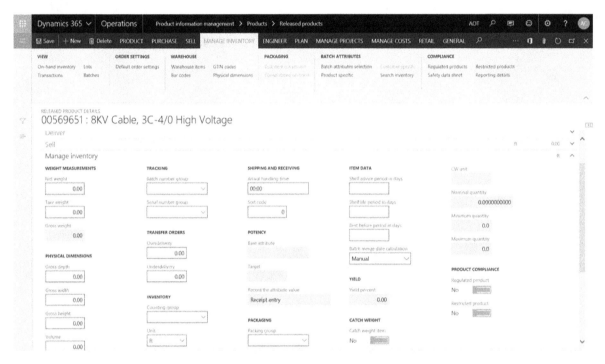

Step 19: Expand Manage inventory fast tab

Next we will need to define some of the default inventory management settings for the product.

To do this we will want to return to the product that you just created and expand out the **Manage Inventory** tab group.

dyn c
www.dynamicscompanions.com
Dynamics Companions

- 56 -

www.blindsquirrelpublishing.com
© 2019 Blind Squirrel Publishing, LLC , All Rights Reserved

BLIND SQUIRREL
PUBLISHING

DYNAMICS COMPANIONS
BARE BONES CONFIGURATION GUIDE

CONFIGURING INVENTORY MANAGEMENT WITHIN DYNAMICS 365 FOR FINANCE & OPERATIONS
MODULE 5: CONFIGURING BATCH AND SERIALIZED PRODUCTS

Creating a Batch Controlled Product

How to do it...

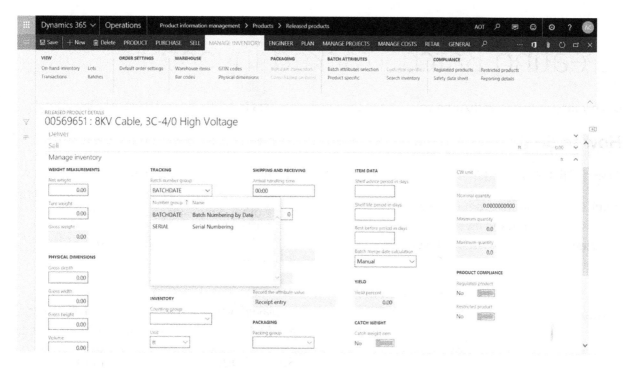

Step 20: Select the Batch number group

Since this product is tracked in batches we will want to assign a tracking number code to the **Batch number group** for the product.

To do this we will just need to select the **Batch number group** from the dropdown list.

For this example, we will want to click on the **Batch number group** dropdown list and select **BATCHDATE**.

dync
www.dynamicscompanions.com
Dynamics Companions

- 57 -

www.blindsquirrelpublishing.com
© 2019 Blind Squirrel Publishing, LLC, All Rights Reserved

BLIND SQUIRREL
PUBLISHING

DYNAMICS COMPANIONS
BARE BONES CONFIGURATION GUIDE

CONFIGURING INVENTORY MANAGEMENT WITHIN DYNAMICS 365 FOR FINANCE & OPERATIONS
MODULE 5: CONFIGURING BATCH AND SERIALIZED PRODUCTS

Creating Batch Tracked Inventory

Once your product is configured you can see the batch numbers in action by creating some inventory.

How to do it...

Step 1: Click On-hand inventory

A quick way to do this from the product itself is to click on the **On Hand Inventory** button within the **View** group of the **Manage Inventory** ribbon bar.

To do this just click on the **On-hand inventory** button.

Step 2: Click Quantity adjustment

This will open up the **On-hand** inventory view for the product and se can create some inventory through the quantity adjustment feature.

To do this just click on the **Quantity adjustment** button.

Step 3: Update the Item number

When the counting form is displayed, we just need to create a new record.

To do this we will just need to update the **Item number** value.

For this example, we will want to set the **Item number** to **00569651**.

Step 4: Click Inventory > Display dimensions

By default you don't see many of the inventory dimensions on this form, so to fix that by adding some other dimensions to our form.

To do this just click on the **Inventory > Display dimensions** button.

When the inventory **Dimensions** selector is displayed, you will see that the **Batch Number** and **Serial Number** dimensions are not enabled.

Step 5: Toggle the Batch number and toggle the Serial number

All we need to do is enable the batch and serial numbers to be shown.

To do this we will just need to toggle the **Batch number** option and toggle the **Serial number** option.

For this example, we will want to click on the **Batch number** toggle switch and set it to the **Checked** value and click on the **Serial number** toggle switch and set it to the **Checked** value.

Step 6: Toggle the Save setup and click OK

Before we finish and exit from the form we will want to save these settings because we will probably want to see these dimensions all of the time.

To do this we will just need to toggle the **Save setup** option and click on the **OK** button.

www.dynamicscompanions.com
Dynamics Companions

- 58 -

www.blindsquirrelpublishing.com
© 2019 Blind Squirrel Publishing, LLC , All Rights Reserved

BLIND SQUIRREL
PUBLISHING

DYNAMICS COMPANIONS
BARE BONES CONFIGURATION GUIDE

CONFIGURING INVENTORY MANAGEMENT WITHIN DYNAMICS 365 FOR FINANCE & OPERATIONS
MODULE 5: CONFIGURING BATCH AND SERIALIZED PRODUCTS

For this example, we will want to click on the **Save setup** toggle switch and set it to the **Yes** value.

Step 7: Update the Site, update the Warehouse and update the Location

While we do the inventory count we will want to specify the location that we are counting the inventory into.

To do this we will just need to update the **Site** value, update the **Warehouse** value and update the **Location** value.

For this example, we will want to set the **Site** to **SD12**, set the **Warehouse** to **120** and set the **Location** to **01-01-1**.

Step 8: Update the Quantity and click OK

And then we will want to specify how much product is in that location.

To do this we will just need to update the **Quantity** value and click on the **OK** button.

For this example, we will want to set the **Quantity** to **1000**.

Step 9: Click Display dimensions

When we return back to the **On-hand** inquiry we will see that the inventory has been created. We don't see any batch numbers though because we have not chosen to view that dimension. So we will want to make a small change to the view and add some dimensions.

To do this just click on the **Display dimensions** button.

This will open up the **Dimension display** panel where we can change the dimensions.

Step 10: Toggle the Warehouse, toggle the Location, toggle the Batch number, toggle the Serial number and click OK

All we need to do now is add a few more dimensions to the display.

To do this we will just need to toggle the **Warehouse** option, toggle the **Location** option, toggle the **Batch number** option, toggle the **Serial number** option and click on the **OK** button.

For this example, we will want to click on the **Warehouse** toggle switch and set it to the **Checked** value, click on the **Location** toggle switch and set it to the **Checked** value, click on the **Batch number** toggle switch and set it to the **Checked** value, click on the **Serial number** toggle switch and set it to the **Checked** value.

Now when you look at the inventory on hand you will see that the **Batch Number** has been automatically assigned to our product.

www.dynamicscompanions.com
Dynamics Companions

- 59 -

www.blindsquirrelpublishing.com
© 2019 Blind Squirrel Publishing, LLC , All Rights Reserved

BLIND SQUIRREL
PUBLISHING

DYNAMICS COMPANIONS
BARE BONES CONFIGURATION GUIDE

CONFIGURING INVENTORY MANAGEMENT WITHIN DYNAMICS 365 FOR FINANCE & OPERATIONS
MODULE 5: CONFIGURING BATCH AND SERIALIZED PRODUCTS

Creating Batch Tracked Inventory

How to do it...

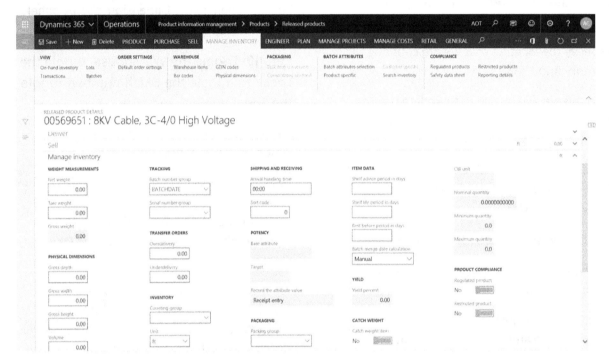

Step 1: Click On-hand inventory

A quick way to do this from the product itself is to click on the **On Hand Inventory** button within the **View** group of the **Manage Inventory** ribbon bar.

To do this just click on the **On-hand inventory** button.

dync
www.dynamicscompanions.com
Dynamics Companions

- 60 -

www.blindsquirrelpublishing.com
© 2019 Blind Squirrel Publishing, LLC , All Rights Reserved

BLIND SQUIRREL
PUBLISHING

DYNAMICS COMPANIONS
BARE BONES CONFIGURATION GUIDE

CONFIGURING INVENTORY MANAGEMENT WITHIN DYNAMICS 365 FOR FINANCE & OPERATIONS
MODULE 5: CONFIGURING BATCH AND SERIALIZED PRODUCTS

Creating Batch Tracked Inventory

How to do it...

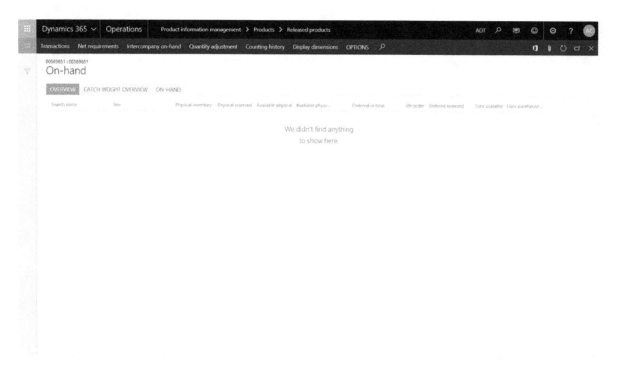

Step 2: Click Quantity adjustment

This will open up the **On-hand** inventory view for the product and se can create some inventory through the quantity adjustment feature.

To do this just click on the **Quantity adjustment** button.

dync
www.dynamicscompanions.com
Dynamics Companions

- 61 -

www.blindsquirrelpublishing.com
© 2019 Blind Squirrel Publishing, LLC , All Rights Reserved

BLIND SQUIRREL
PUBLISHING

DYNAMICS COMPANIONS
BARE BONES CONFIGURATION GUIDE

CONFIGURING INVENTORY MANAGEMENT WITHIN DYNAMICS 365 FOR FINANCE & OPERATIONS
MODULE 5: CONFIGURING BATCH AND SERIALIZED PRODUCTS

Creating Batch Tracked Inventory

How to do it...

Step 3: Update the Item number

When the counting form is displayed, we just need to create a new record.

To do this we will just need to update the **Item number** value.

For this example, we will want to set the **Item number** to **00569651**.

www.dynamicscompanions.com
Dynamics Companions

- 62 -

www.blindsquirrelpublishing.com
© 2019 Blind Squirrel Publishing, LLC , All Rights Reserved

BLIND SQUIRREL
PUBLISHING

DYNAMICS COMPANIONS
BARE BONES CONFIGURATION GUIDE

CONFIGURING INVENTORY MANAGEMENT WITHIN DYNAMICS 365 FOR FINANCE & OPERATIONS
MODULE 5: CONFIGURING BATCH AND SERIALIZED PRODUCTS

Creating Batch Tracked Inventory

How to do it...

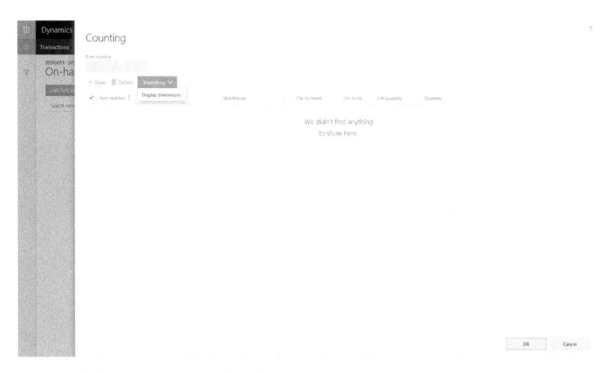

Step 4: Click Inventory > Display dimensions

By default you don't see many of the inventory dimensions on this form, so to fix that by adding some other dimensions to our form.

To do this just click on the **Inventory > Display dimensions** button.

DYNAMICS COMPANIONS
BARE BONES CONFIGURATION GUIDE

CONFIGURING INVENTORY MANAGEMENT WITHIN DYNAMICS 365 FOR FINANCE & OPERATIONS
MODULE 5: CONFIGURING BATCH AND SERIALIZED PRODUCTS

Creating Batch Tracked Inventory

How to do it...

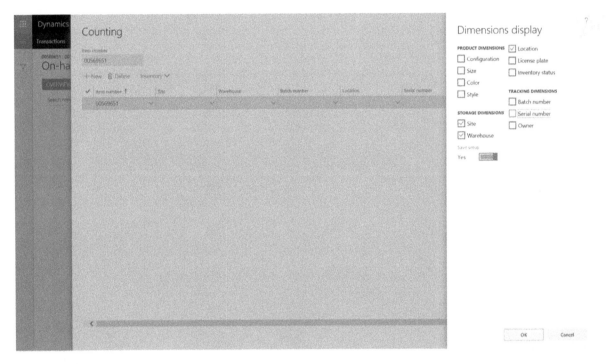

Step 4: Click Inventory > Display dimensions

When the inventory **Dimensions** selector is displayed, you will see that the **Batch Number** and **Serial Number** dimensions are not enabled.

dyn c
www.dynamicscompanions.com
Dynamics Companions

- 64 -

www.blindsquirrelpublishing.com
© 2019 Blind Squirrel Publishing, LLC , All Rights Reserved

BLIND SQUIRREL
PUBLISHING

DYNAMICS COMPANIONS
BARE BONES CONFIGURATION GUIDE

CONFIGURING INVENTORY MANAGEMENT WITHIN DYNAMICS 365 FOR FINANCE & OPERATIONS
MODULE 5: CONFIGURING BATCH AND SERIALIZED PRODUCTS

Creating Batch Tracked Inventory

How to do it...

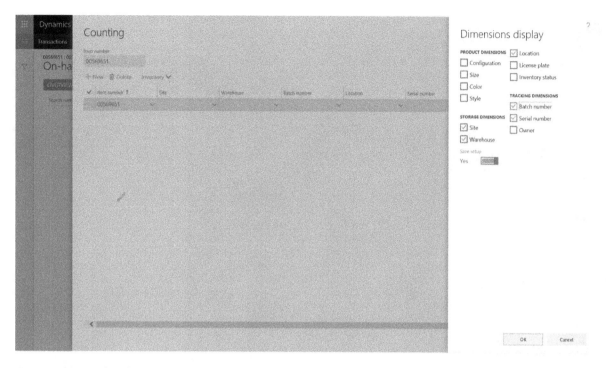

Step 5: Toggle the Batch number and toggle the Serial number

All we need to do is enable the batch and serial numbers to be shown.

To do this we will just need to toggle the **Batch number** option and toggle the **Serial number** option.

For this example, we will want to click on the **Batch number** toggle switch and set it to the **Checked** value and click on the **Serial number** toggle switch and set it to the **Checked** value.

www.dynamicscompanions.com
Dynamics Companions

- 65 -

www.blindsquirrelpublishing.com
© 2019 Blind Squirrel Publishing, LLC , All Rights Reserved

BLIND SQUIRREL
PUBLISHING

DYNAMICS COMPANIONS
BARE BONES CONFIGURATION GUIDE

CONFIGURING INVENTORY MANAGEMENT WITHIN DYNAMICS 365 FOR FINANCE & OPERATIONS
MODULE 5: CONFIGURING BATCH AND SERIALIZED PRODUCTS

Creating Batch Tracked Inventory

How to do it...

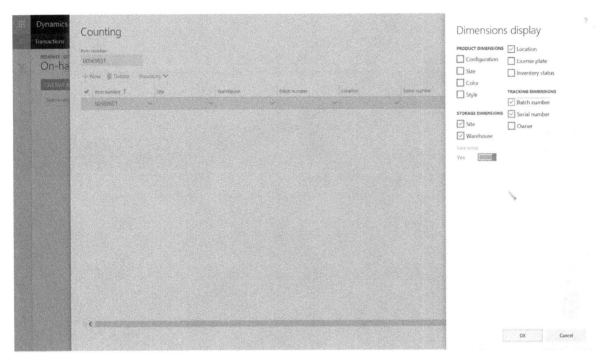

Step 6: Toggle the Save setup and click OK

Before we finish and exit from the form we will want to save these settings because we will probably want to see these dimensions all of the time.

To do this we will just need to toggle the **Save setup** option and click on the **OK** button.

For this example, we will want to click on the **Save setup** toggle switch and set it to the **Yes** value.

dyn c
www.dynamicscompanions.com
Dynamics Companions

- 66 -

www.blindsquirrelpublishing.com
© 2019 Blind Squirrel Publishing, LLC , All Rights Reserved

BLIND SQUIRREL
PUBLISHING

DYNAMICS COMPANIONS
BARE BONES CONFIGURATION GUIDE

CONFIGURING INVENTORY MANAGEMENT WITHIN DYNAMICS 365 FOR FINANCE & OPERATIONS
MODULE 5: CONFIGURING BATCH AND SERIALIZED PRODUCTS

Creating Batch Tracked Inventory

How to do it...

Step 7: Update the Site, update the Warehouse and update the Location

While we do the inventory count we will want to specify the location that we are counting the inventory into.

To do this we will just need to update the **Site** value, update the **Warehouse** value and update the **Location** value.

For this example, we will want to set the **Site** to **SD12**, set the **Warehouse** to **120** and set the **Location** to **01-01-1**.

dync

www.dynamicscompanions.com
Dynamics Companions

- 67 -

www.blindsquirrelpublishing.com
© 2019 Blind Squirrel Publishing, LLC, All Rights Reserved

BLIND SQUIRREL
PUBLISHING

DYNAMICS COMPANIONS
BARE BONES CONFIGURATION GUIDE

CONFIGURING INVENTORY MANAGEMENT WITHIN DYNAMICS 365 FOR FINANCE & OPERATIONS
MODULE 5: CONFIGURING BATCH AND SERIALIZED PRODUCTS

Creating Batch Tracked Inventory

How to do it...

Step 8: Update the Quantity and click OK

And then we will want to specify how much product is in that location.

To do this we will just need to update the **Quantity** value and click on the **OK** button.

For this example, we will want to set the **Quantity** to **1000**.

www.dynamicscompanions.com
Dynamics Companions

- 68 -

www.blindsquirrelpublishing.com
© 2019 Blind Squirrel Publishing, LLC , All Rights Reserved

BLIND SQUIRREL
PUBLISHING

DYNAMICS COMPANIONS
BARE BONES CONFIGURATION GUIDE

CONFIGURING INVENTORY MANAGEMENT WITHIN DYNAMICS 365 FOR FINANCE & OPERATIONS
MODULE 5: CONFIGURING BATCH AND SERIALIZED PRODUCTS

Creating Batch Tracked Inventory

How to do it...

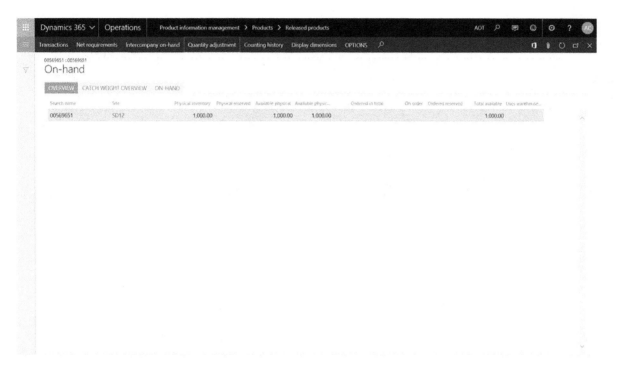

Step 9: Click Display dimensions

When we return back to the **On-hand** inquiry we will see that the inventory has been created. We don't see any batch numbers though because we have not chosen to view that dimension. So we will want to make a small change to the view and add some dimensions.

To do this just click on the **Display dimensions** button.

dync
www.dynamicscompanions.com
Dynamics Companions

- 69 -

www.blindsquirrelpublishing.com
© 2019 Blind Squirrel Publishing, LLC , All Rights Reserved

BLIND SQUIRREL
PUBLISHING

DYNAMICS COMPANIONS
BARE BONES CONFIGURATION GUIDE

CONFIGURING INVENTORY MANAGEMENT WITHIN DYNAMICS 365 FOR FINANCE & OPERATIONS
MODULE 5: CONFIGURING BATCH AND SERIALIZED PRODUCTS

Creating Batch Tracked Inventory

How to do it...

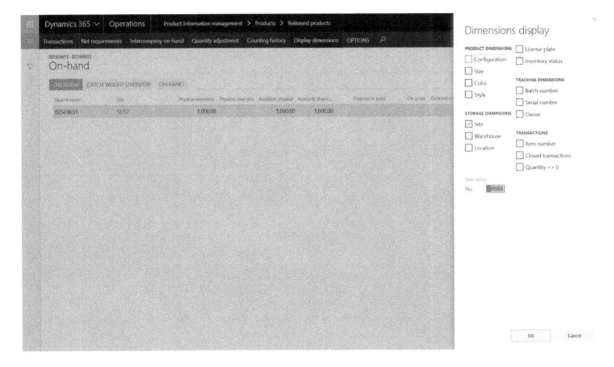

Step 9: Click Display dimensions

This will open up the **Dimension display** panel where we can change the dimensions.

DYNAMICS COMPANIONS
BARE BONES CONFIGURATION GUIDE

CONFIGURING INVENTORY MANAGEMENT WITHIN DYNAMICS 365 FOR FINANCE & OPERATIONS
MODULE 5: CONFIGURING BATCH AND SERIALIZED PRODUCTS

Creating Batch Tracked Inventory

How to do it...

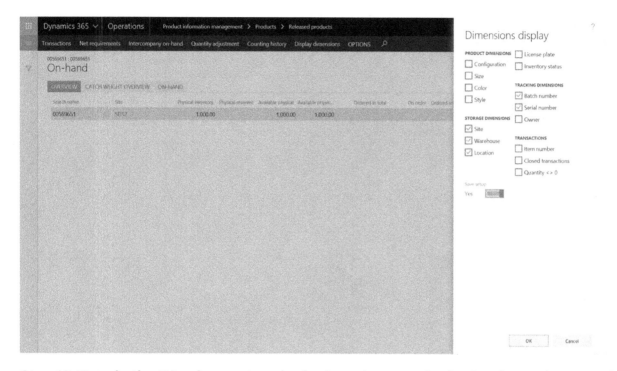

Step 10: Toggle the Warehouse, toggle the Location, toggle the Batch number, toggle the Serial number and click OK

All we need to do now is add a few more dimensions to the display.

To do this we will just need to toggle the **Warehouse** option, toggle the **Location** option, toggle the **Batch number** option, toggle the **Serial number** option and click on the **OK** button.

For this example, we will want to click on the **Warehouse** toggle switch and set it to the **Checked** value, click on the **Location** toggle switch and set it to the **Checked** value, click on the **Batch number** toggle switch and set it to the **Checked** value, click on the **Serial number** toggle switch and set it to the **Checked** value.

dynᴄ   www.dynamicscompanions.com
Dynamics Companions

- 71 -

www.blindsquirrelpublishing.com
© 2019 Blind Squirrel Publishing, LLC , All Rights Reserved

BLIND SQUIRREL
PUBLISHING

DYNAMICS COMPANIONS
BARE BONES CONFIGURATION GUIDE

CONFIGURING INVENTORY MANAGEMENT WITHIN DYNAMICS 365 FOR FINANCE & OPERATIONS
MODULE 5: CONFIGURING BATCH AND SERIALIZED PRODUCTS

Creating Batch Tracked Inventory

How to do it...

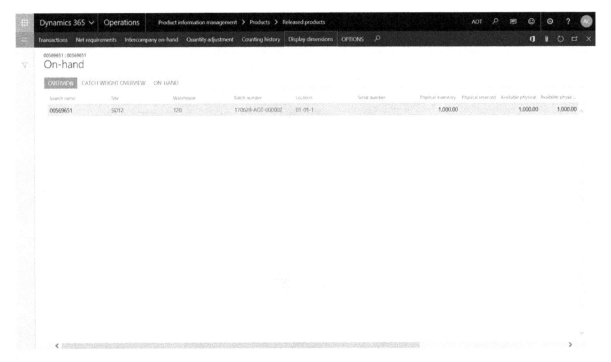

Step 10: Toggle the Warehouse, toggle the Location, toggle the Batch number, toggle the Serial number and click OK

Now when you look at the inventory on hand you will see that the **Batch Number** has been automatically assigned to our product.

dyn c
www.dynamicscompanions.com
Dynamics Companions

- 72 -

www.blindsquirrelpublishing.com
© 2019 Blind Squirrel Publishing, LLC , All Rights Reserved

BLIND SQUIRREL
PUBLISHING

DYNAMICS COMPANIONS
BARE BONES CONFIGURATION GUIDE

CONFIGURING INVENTORY MANAGEMENT WITHIN DYNAMICS 365 FOR FINANCE & OPERATIONS
MODULE 5: CONFIGURING BATCH AND SERIALIZED PRODUCTS

Viewing Batch Details

There is another way that you can view the batch details, and that is directly through the **Released Product** details page.

How to do it...

Step 1: Click Batches

So when we return back to the released products form we will want to open up the batch information for the product.

To do this just click on the **Batches** button.

This will open up a list of all of the batches that you have created for this product. Notice also that the batches are date controlled and through here you are also able to update the **Expiration Dates**.

When you are done, just click on the **Close** button to exit from the form.

DYNAMICS COMPANIONS
BARE BONES CONFIGURATION GUIDE

CONFIGURING INVENTORY MANAGEMENT WITHIN DYNAMICS 365 FOR FINANCE & OPERATIONS
MODULE 5: CONFIGURING BATCH AND SERIALIZED PRODUCTS

Viewing Batch Details

How to do it...

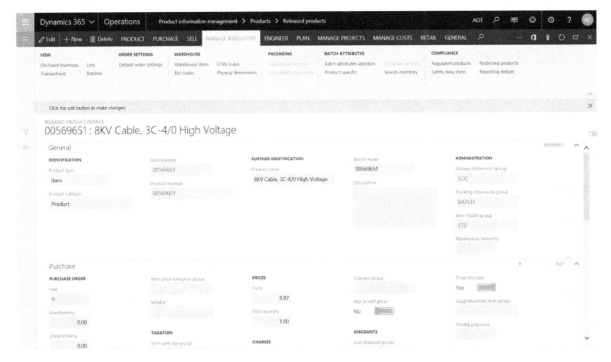

Step 1: Click Batches

So when we return back to the released products form we will want to open up the batch information for the product.

To do this just click on the **Batches** button.

www.dynamicscompanions.com
Dynamics Companions

- 74 -

www.blindsquirrelpublishing.com
© 2019 Blind Squirrel Publishing, LLC , All Rights Reserved

BLIND SQUIRREL
PUBLISHING

DYNAMICS COMPANIONS
BARE BONES CONFIGURATION GUIDE

CONFIGURING INVENTORY MANAGEMENT WITHIN DYNAMICS 365 FOR FINANCE & OPERATIONS
MODULE 5: CONFIGURING BATCH AND SERIALIZED PRODUCTS

Viewing Batch Details

How to do it...

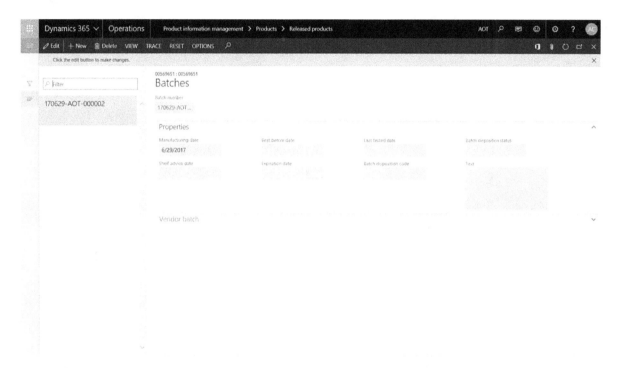

Step 1: Click Batches

This will open up a list of all of the batches that you have created for this product. Notice also that the batches are date controlled and through here you are also able to update the **Expiration Dates**.

When you are done, just click on the **Close** button to exit from the form.

dyn c

www.dynamicscompanions.com
Dynamics Companions

- 75 -

www.blindsquirrelpublishing.com
© 2019 Blind Squirrel Publishing, LLC , All Rights Reserved

BLIND SQUIRREL
PUBLISHING

DYNAMICS COMPANIONS
BARE BONES CONFIGURATION GUIDE

CONFIGURING INVENTORY MANAGEMENT WITHIN DYNAMICS 365 FOR FINANCE & OPERATIONS
MODULE 5: CONFIGURING BATCH AND SERIALIZED PRODUCTS

Viewing Batch Details

Review

How easy was that. Now we have a product that we are tracking by batch id within the system.

DYNAMICS COMPANIONS
BARE BONES CONFIGURATION GUIDE

CONFIGURING INVENTORY MANAGEMENT WITHIN DYNAMICS 365 FOR FINANCE & OPERATIONS
MODULE 5: CONFIGURING BATCH AND SERIALIZED PRODUCTS

Configuring A Serialized Product

Additionally you can create products that are serialized.

Topics Covered

- Creating a Serial Tracked Product

- Creating Serial Tracked Inventory

 www.dynamicscompanions.com
Dynamics Companions

- 77 -

www.blindsquirrelpublishing.com
© 2019 Blind Squirrel Publishing, LLC , All Rights Reserved

BLIND SQUIRREL
PUBLISHING

DYNAMICS COMPANIONS
BARE BONES CONFIGURATION GUIDE

CONFIGURING INVENTORY MANAGEMENT WITHIN DYNAMICS 365 FOR FINANCE & OPERATIONS
MODULE 5: CONFIGURING BATCH AND SERIALIZED PRODUCTS

Creating a Serial Tracked Product

Since none of the products that we have created so far are serialized products we will want to quickly create a new product that has serial number tracking configured on it.

How to do it...

Step 1: Click New

We will want to open up the Released products form an create a new product.

To do this just click on the **New** button.

Step 2: Update the Product number

This will open up the **New released product** form and we will want to give our new product a number to identify it.

To do this we will just need to update the **Product number** value.

For this example, we will want to set the **Product number** to **47250739**.

Step 3: Update the Product name

We will then want to give our product a more descriptive name.

To do this we will just need to update the **Product name** value.

For this example, we will want to set the **Product name** to **ZP-4116-3GL Pype Contact Unit**.

Step 4: Select the Item model group

Next we will want to assign the product to an Item model group.

To do this we will just need to select the **Item model group** from the dropdown list.

For this example, we will want to click on the **Item model group** dropdown list and select **STD**.

Step 5: Update the Item gropu

And next we will associate the product with an Item group.

To do this we will just need to update the **Item gropu** value.

For this example, we will want to set the **Item gropu** to **DEFAULT**.

Step 6: Update the Storage dimension group

We will now want to tell the system how we are going to store this product and to what level.

To do this we will just need to update the **Storage dimension group** value.

For this example, we will want to set the **Storage dimension group** to **LOC**.

Step 7: Select the Product tracking Dimension

DYNAMICS COMPANIONS
BARE BONES CONFIGURATION GUIDE

CONFIGURING INVENTORY MANAGEMENT WITHIN DYNAMICS 365 FOR FINANCE & OPERATIONS
MODULE 5: CONFIGURING BATCH AND SERIALIZED PRODUCTS

And now we can specify that the product is being tracked by serial number.

To do this we will just need to select the **Product tracking Dimension** from the dropdown list.

For this example, we will want to click on the **Product tracking Dimension** dropdown list and select **SERIAL**.

Step 8: Update the Inventory unit

Now we will want to assign our product some units of measure. We will start off by selecting and Inventory unit of measure.

To do this we will just need to update the **Inventory unit** value.

For this example, we will want to set the **Inventory unit** to **ea**.

Step 9: Update the Purchase unit

Next we will want to select a unit of measure to purchase the products in.

To do this we will just need to update the **Purchase unit** value.

For this example, we will want to set the **Purchase unit** to **ea**.

Step 10: Update the Sales unit

We can now select a unit of measure that we will sell the product in.

To do this we will just need to update the **Sales unit** value.

For this example, we will want to set the **Sales unit** to **ea**.

Step 11: Update the BOM unit

And finally we will want to select a unit of measure that we will use for all of our production an engineering configurations.

To do this we will just need to update the **BOM unit** value.

For this example, we will want to set the **BOM unit** to **ea**.

Step 12: Click OK

Now we can create the product.

To do this just click on the **OK** button.

This will open up the larger Released product configuration form where we will want to make a couple of other settings for the product.

Step 13: Expand the Manage inventory fast tab

We will start off within the manage inventory section of the configuration.

To do this we will scroll down the form to the **Manage inventory** fast tab and expand it.

Step 14: Update the Seial number group

Now we will want to specify the way that we want the serial numbers to be formatted.

To do this we will just need to update the **Seial number group** value.

For this example, we will want to set the **Seial number group** to **SERIAL**.

Step 15: Select the Caluculation group

Next we will want to expand the **Engineer** fast tab and assign our product to a calculation group.

To do this we will just need to select the **Caluculation group** from the dropdown list.

For this example, we will want to click on the **Caluculation group** dropdown list and select **DEFAULT**.

Step 16: Update the Price

www.dynamicscompanions.com
Dynamics Companions

- 79 -

www.blindsquirrelpublishing.com
© 2019 Blind Squirrel Publishing, LLC , All Rights Reserved

BLIND SQUIRREL
PUBLISHING

DYNAMICS COMPANIONS
BARE BONES CONFIGURATION GUIDE

CONFIGURING INVENTORY MANAGEMENT WITHIN DYNAMICS 365 FOR FINANCE & OPERATIONS
MODULE 5: CONFIGURING BATCH AND SERIALIZED PRODUCTS

And then we will want to tell the system how much the product costs to purchase.

To do this we will just need to update the **Price** value.

For this example, we will want to set the **Price** to **47.58**.

Step 17: Click Item price

Step 18: Click Calculate item cost

When the **Item price** form is displayed we will be able ro calculate the prices from the purchase cost.

To do this just click on the **Calculate item cost** button.

This will open up the **Calculation for an item** form and we will be able to tell it what we want the cost to be associated to.

Step 19: Select the Costing version

We will start by selecting the costing version that we want the cost to be linked to.

To do this we will just need to select the **Costing version** from the dropdown list.

For this example, we will want to click on the **Costing version** dropdown list and select **STD**.

Step 20: Select the Site

And then we will select the site that we want the cost to be linked to.

To do this we will just need to select the **Site** from the dropdown list.

For this example, we will want to click on the **Site** dropdown list and select **SD12**.

Step 21: Click OK

After we have done that we can get the system to calculate the price for us.

To do this just click on the **OK** button.

Step 22: Click Activate pending prices

When we return to the **Item prices** form we will see that the price has been calculated and we just need to activate the cost.

To do this just click on the **Activate pending prices** button.

DYNAMICS COMPANIONS
BARE BONES CONFIGURATION GUIDE

CONFIGURING INVENTORY MANAGEMENT WITHIN DYNAMICS 365 FOR FINANCE & OPERATIONS
MODULE 5: CONFIGURING BATCH AND SERIALIZED PRODUCTS

Creating a Serial Tracked Product

How to do it...

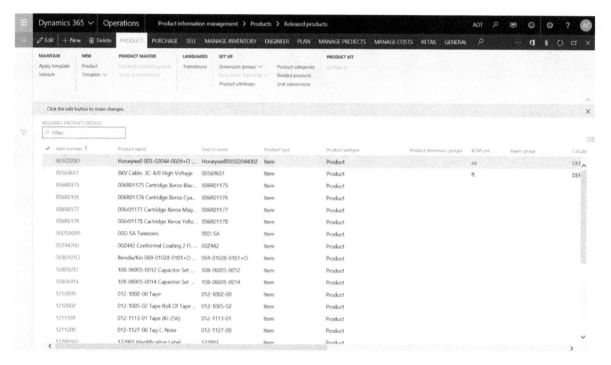

Step 1: Click New

We will want to open up the Released products form an create a new product.

To do this just click on the **New** button.

www.dynamicscompanions.com
Dynamics Companions

- 81 -

www.blindsquirrelpublishing.com
© 2019 Blind Squirrel Publishing, LLC , All Rights Reserved

BLIND SQUIRREL
PUBLISHING

DYNAMICS COMPANIONS
BARE BONES CONFIGURATION GUIDE

CONFIGURING INVENTORY MANAGEMENT WITHIN DYNAMICS 365 FOR FINANCE & OPERATIONS
MODULE 5: CONFIGURING BATCH AND SERIALIZED PRODUCTS

Creating a Serial Tracked Product

How to do it...

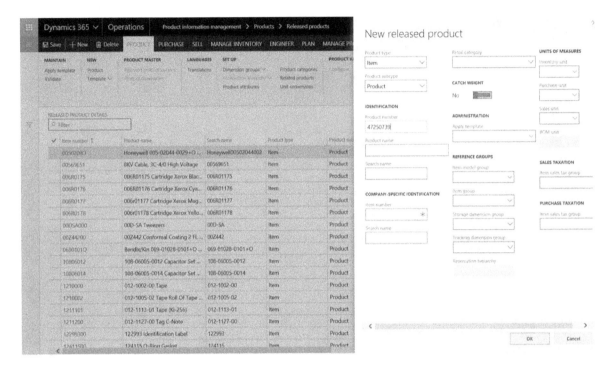

Step 2: Update the Product number

This will open up the **New released product** form and we will want to give our new product a number to identify it.

To do this we will just need to update the **Product number** value.

For this example, we will want to set the **Product number** to **47250739**.

dync
www.dynamicscompanions.com
Dynamics Companions

- 82 -

www.blindsquirrelpublishing.com
© 2019 Blind Squirrel Publishing, LLC , All Rights Reserved

BLIND SQUIRREL
PUBLISHING

DYNAMICS COMPANIONS
BARE BONES CONFIGURATION GUIDE

CONFIGURING INVENTORY MANAGEMENT WITHIN DYNAMICS 365 FOR FINANCE & OPERATIONS
MODULE 5: CONFIGURING BATCH AND SERIALIZED PRODUCTS

Creating a Serial Tracked Product

How to do it...

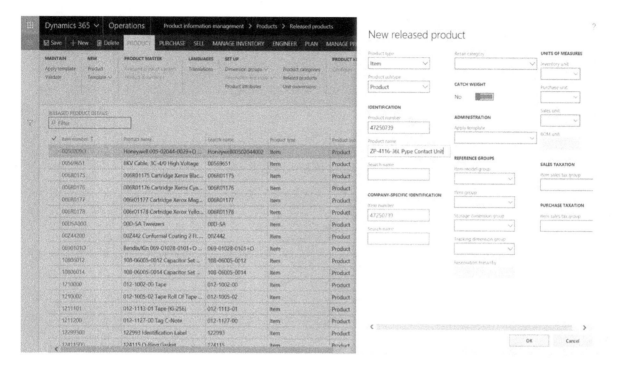

Step 3: Update the Product name

We will then want to give our product a more descriptive name.

To do this we will just need to update the **Product name** value.

For this example, we will want to set the **Product name** to **ZP-4116-3GL Pype Contact Unit**.

www.dynamicscompanions.com
Dynamics Companions

- 83 -

www.blindsquirrelpublishing.com
© 2019 Blind Squirrel Publishing, LLC, All Rights Reserved

BLIND SQUIRREL
PUBLISHING

DYNAMICS COMPANIONS
BARE BONES CONFIGURATION GUIDE

CONFIGURING INVENTORY MANAGEMENT WITHIN DYNAMICS 365 FOR FINANCE & OPERATIONS
MODULE 5: CONFIGURING BATCH AND SERIALIZED PRODUCTS

Creating a Serial Tracked Product

How to do it...

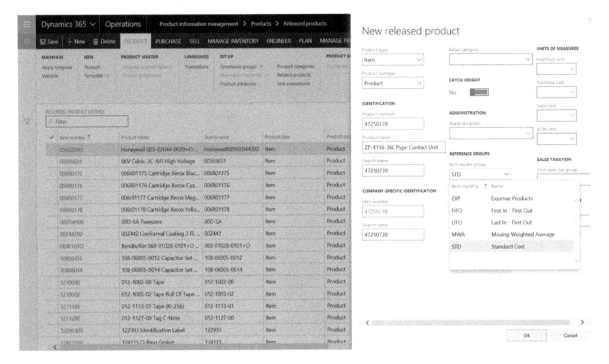

Step 4: Select the Item model group

Next we will want to assign the product to an Item model group.

To do this we will just need to select the **Item model group** from the dropdown list.

For this example, we will want to click on the **Item model group** dropdown list and select **STD**.

dyn c
www.dynamicscompanions.com
Dynamics Companions

- 84 -

www.blindsquirrelpublishing.com
© 2019 Blind Squirrel Publishing, LLC , All Rights Reserved

BLIND SQUIRREL
PUBLISHING

DYNAMICS COMPANIONS
BARE BONES CONFIGURATION GUIDE

CONFIGURING INVENTORY MANAGEMENT WITHIN DYNAMICS 365 FOR FINANCE & OPERATIONS
MODULE 5: CONFIGURING BATCH AND SERIALIZED PRODUCTS

Creating a Serial Tracked Product

How to do it...

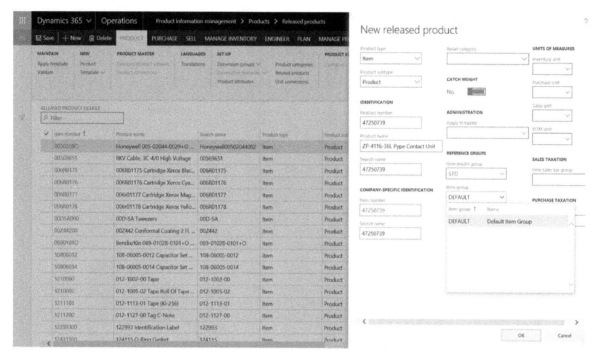

Step 5: Update the Item gropu

And next we will associate the product with an Item group.

To do this we will just need to update the **Item gropu** value.

For this example, we will want to set the **Item gropu** to **DEFAULT**.

DYNAMICS COMPANIONS
BARE BONES CONFIGURATION GUIDE

CONFIGURING INVENTORY MANAGEMENT WITHIN DYNAMICS 365 FOR FINANCE & OPERATIONS
MODULE 5: CONFIGURING BATCH AND SERIALIZED PRODUCTS

Creating a Serial Tracked Product

How to do it...

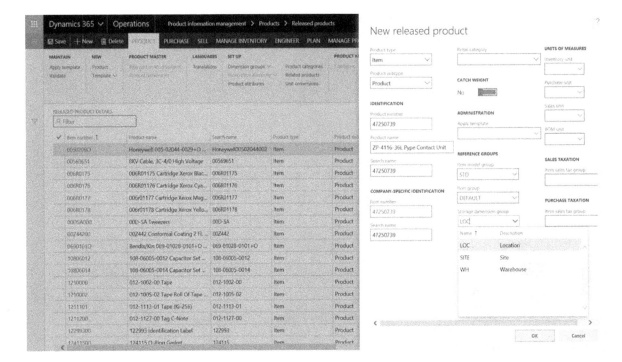

Step 6: Update the Storage dimension group

We will now want to tell the system how we are going to store this product and to what level.

To do this we will just need to update the **Storage dimension group** value.

For this example, we will want to set the **Storage dimension group** to **LOC**.

www.dynamicscompanions.com
Dynamics Companions

- 86 -

www.blindsquirrelpublishing.com
© 2019 Blind Squirrel Publishing, LLC , All Rights Reserved

BLIND SQUIRREL
PUBLISHING

DYNAMICS COMPANIONS
BARE BONES CONFIGURATION GUIDE

CONFIGURING INVENTORY MANAGEMENT WITHIN DYNAMICS 365 FOR FINANCE & OPERATIONS
MODULE 5: CONFIGURING BATCH AND SERIALIZED PRODUCTS

Creating a Serial Tracked Product

How to do it...

Step 7: Select the Product tracking Dimension

And now we can specify that the product is being tracked by serial number.

To do this we will just need to select the **Product tracking Dimension** from the dropdown list.

For this example, we will want to click on the **Product tracking Dimension** dropdown list and select **SERIAL**.

DYNAMICS COMPANIONS
BARE BONES CONFIGURATION GUIDE

CONFIGURING INVENTORY MANAGEMENT WITHIN DYNAMICS 365 FOR FINANCE & OPERATIONS
MODULE 5: CONFIGURING BATCH AND SERIALIZED PRODUCTS

Creating a Serial Tracked Product

How to do it...

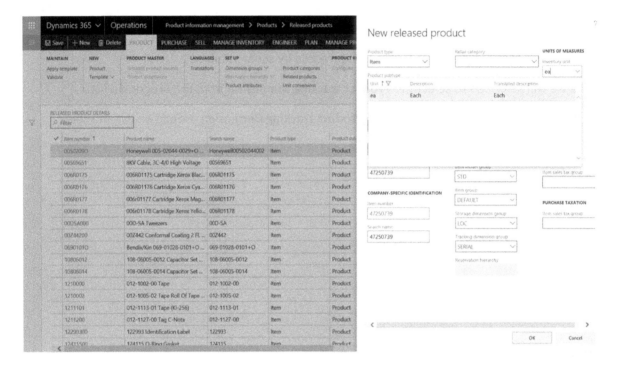

Step 8: Update the Inventory unit

Now we will want to assign our product some units of measure. We will start off by selecting and Inventory unit of measure.

To do this we will just need to update the **Inventory unit** value.

For this example, we will want to set the **Inventory unit** to **ea**.

DYNAMICS COMPANIONS
BARE BONES CONFIGURATION GUIDE

CONFIGURING INVENTORY MANAGEMENT WITHIN DYNAMICS 365 FOR FINANCE & OPERATIONS
MODULE 5: CONFIGURING BATCH AND SERIALIZED PRODUCTS

Creating a Serial Tracked Product

How to do it...

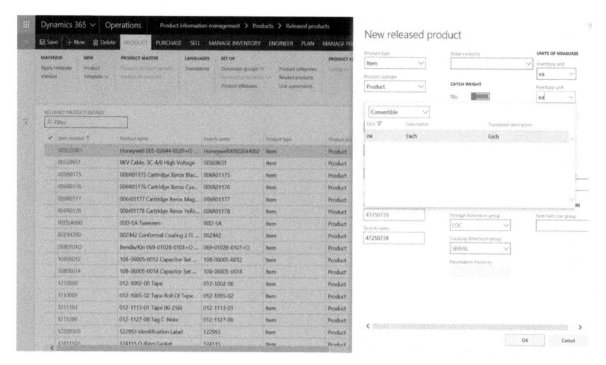

Step 9: Update the Purchase unit

Next we will want to select a unit of measure to purchase the products in.

To do this we will just need to update the **Purchase unit** value.

For this example, we will want to set the **Purchase unit** to **ea**.

dyn c
www.dynamicscompanions.com
Dynamics Companions

- 89 -

www.blindsquirrelpublishing.com
© 2019 Blind Squirrel Publishing, LLC , All Rights Reserved

BLIND SQUIRREL
PUBLISHING

DYNAMICS COMPANIONS
BARE BONES CONFIGURATION GUIDE

CONFIGURING INVENTORY MANAGEMENT WITHIN DYNAMICS 365 FOR FINANCE & OPERATIONS
MODULE 5: CONFIGURING BATCH AND SERIALIZED PRODUCTS

Creating a Serial Tracked Product

How to do it...

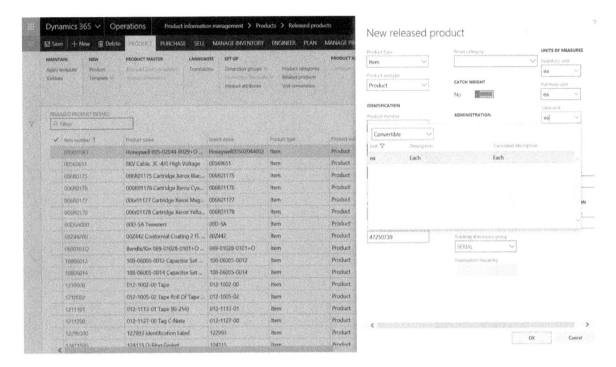

Step 10: Update the Sales unit

We can now select a unit of measure that we will sell the product in.

To do this we will just need to update the **Sales unit** value.

For this example, we will want to set the **Sales unit** to **ea**.

dync
www.dynamicscompanions.com
Dynamics Companions

- 90 -

www.blindsquirrelpublishing.com
© 2019 Blind Squirrel Publishing, LLC , All Rights Reserved

BLIND SQUIRREL
PUBLISHING

DYNAMICS COMPANIONS
BARE BONES CONFIGURATION GUIDE

CONFIGURING INVENTORY MANAGEMENT WITHIN DYNAMICS 365 FOR FINANCE & OPERATIONS
MODULE 5: CONFIGURING BATCH AND SERIALIZED PRODUCTS

Creating a Serial Tracked Product

How to do it...

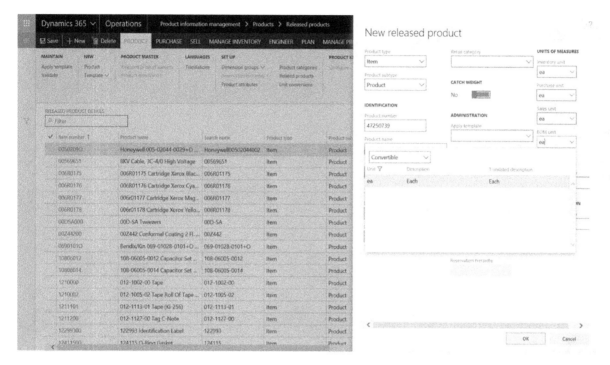

Step 11: Update the BOM unit

And finally we will want to select a unit of measure that we will use for all of our production an engineering configurations.

To do this we will just need to update the **BOM unit** value.

For this example, we will want to set the **BOM unit** to **ea**.

DYNAMICS COMPANIONS
BARE BONES CONFIGURATION GUIDE

CONFIGURING INVENTORY MANAGEMENT WITHIN DYNAMICS 365 FOR FINANCE & OPERATIONS
MODULE 5: CONFIGURING BATCH AND SERIALIZED PRODUCTS

Creating a Serial Tracked Product

How to do it...

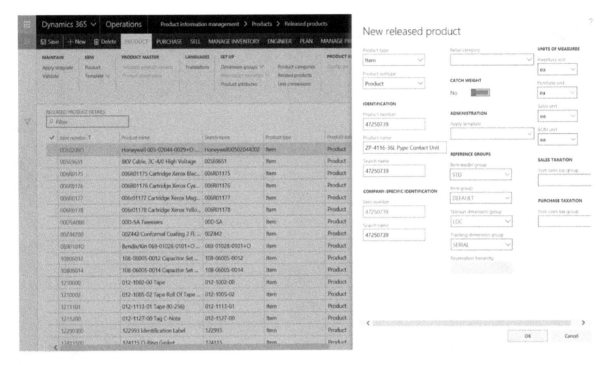

Step 12: Click OK

Now we can create the product.

To do this just click on the **OK** button.

dyn c
www.dynamicscompanions.com
Dynamics Companions

- 92 -

www.blindsquirrelpublishing.com
© 2019 Blind Squirrel Publishing, LLC , All Rights Reserved

BLIND SQUIRREL
PUBLISHING

DYNAMICS COMPANIONS
BARE BONES CONFIGURATION GUIDE

CONFIGURING INVENTORY MANAGEMENT WITHIN DYNAMICS 365 FOR FINANCE & OPERATIONS
MODULE 5: CONFIGURING BATCH AND SERIALIZED PRODUCTS

Creating a Serial Tracked Product

How to do it...

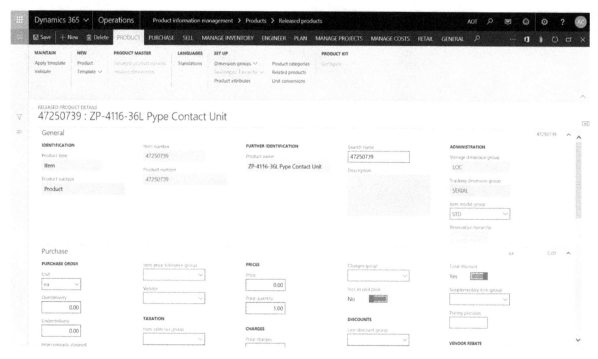

Step 12: Click OK

This will open up the larger Released product configuration form where we will want to make a couple of other settings for the product.

dync
Dynamics Companions

www.dynamicscompanions.com
Dynamics Companions

- 93 -

www.blindsquirrelpublishing.com
© 2019 Blind Squirrel Publishing, LLC, All Rights Reserved

BLIND SQUIRREL
PUBLISHING

DYNAMICS COMPANIONS
BARE BONES CONFIGURATION GUIDE

CONFIGURING INVENTORY MANAGEMENT WITHIN DYNAMICS 365 FOR FINANCE & OPERATIONS
MODULE 5: CONFIGURING BATCH AND SERIALIZED PRODUCTS

Creating a Serial Tracked Product

How to do it...

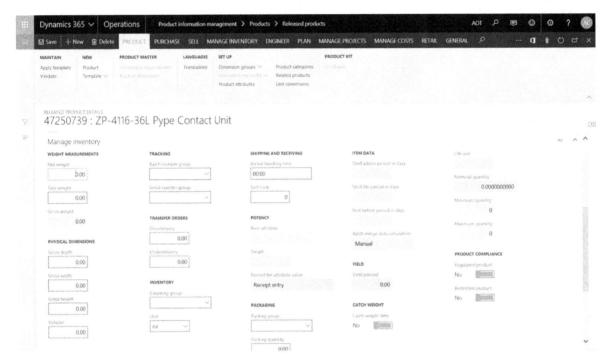

Step 13: Expand the Manage inventory fast tab

We will start off within the manage inventory section of the configuration.

To do this we will scroll down the form to the **Manage inventory** fast tab and expand it.

dync
www.dynamicscompanions.com
Dynamics Companions

- 94 -

www.blindsquirrelpublishing.com
© 2019 Blind Squirrel Publishing, LLC , All Rights Reserved

BLIND SQUIRREL
PUBLISHING

DYNAMICS COMPANIONS
BARE BONES CONFIGURATION GUIDE

CONFIGURING INVENTORY MANAGEMENT WITHIN DYNAMICS 365 FOR FINANCE & OPERATIONS
MODULE 5: CONFIGURING BATCH AND SERIALIZED PRODUCTS

Creating a Serial Tracked Product

How to do it...

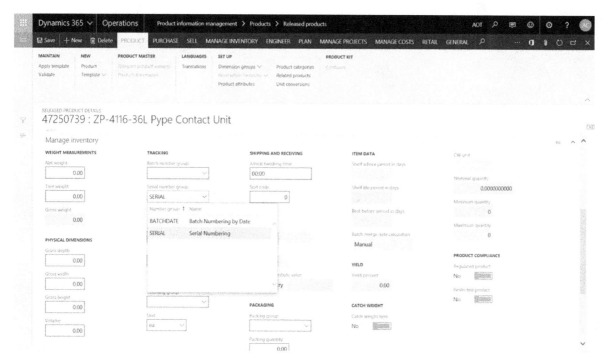

Step 14: Update the Seial number group

Now we will want to specify the way that we want the serial numbers to be formatted.

To do this we will just need to update the **Seial number group** value.

For this example, we will want to set the **Seial number group** to **SERIAL**.

dync
www.dynamicscompanions.com
Dynamics Companions

- 95 -

www.blindsquirrelpublishing.com
© 2019 Blind Squirrel Publishing, LLC, All Rights Reserved

BLIND SQUIRREL
PUBLISHING

DYNAMICS COMPANIONS
BARE BONES CONFIGURATION GUIDE

CONFIGURING INVENTORY MANAGEMENT WITHIN DYNAMICS 365 FOR FINANCE & OPERATIONS
MODULE 5: CONFIGURING BATCH AND SERIALIZED PRODUCTS

Creating a Serial Tracked Product

How to do it...

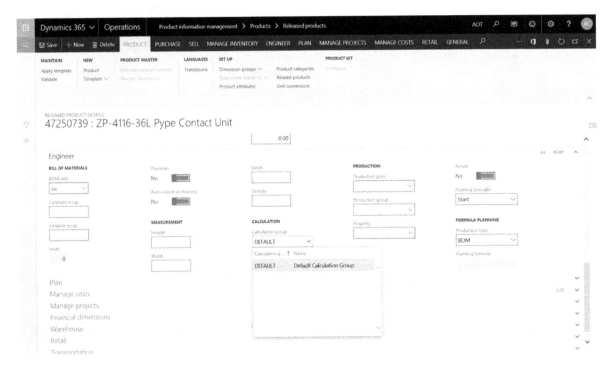

Step 15: Select the Caluculation group

Next we will want to expand the **Engineer** fast tab and assign our product to a calculation group.

To do this we will just need to select the **Caluculation group** from the dropdown list.

For this example, we will want to click on the **Caluculation group** dropdown list and select **DEFAULT**.

DYNAMICS COMPANIONS
BARE BONES CONFIGURATION GUIDE

CONFIGURING INVENTORY MANAGEMENT WITHIN DYNAMICS 365 FOR FINANCE & OPERATIONS
MODULE 5: CONFIGURING BATCH AND SERIALIZED PRODUCTS

Creating a Serial Tracked Product

How to do it...

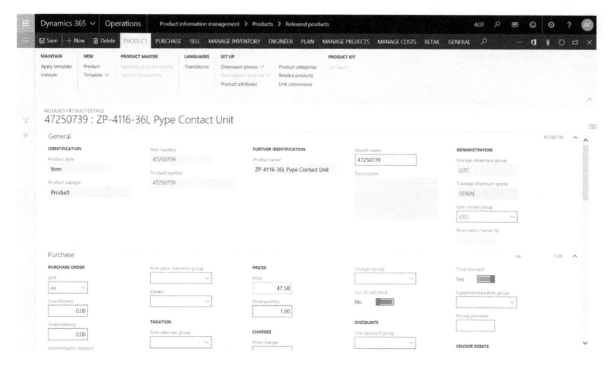

Step 16: Update the Price

And then we will want to tell the system how much the product costs to purchase.

To do this we will just need to update the **Price** value.

For this example, we will want to set the **Price** to **47.58**.

dyn c
www.dynamicscompanions.com
Dynamics Companions

- 97 -

www.blindsquirrelpublishing.com
© 2019 Blind Squirrel Publishing, LLC , All Rights Reserved

BLIND SQUIRREL
PUBLISHING

DYNAMICS COMPANIONS
BARE BONES CONFIGURATION GUIDE

CONFIGURING INVENTORY MANAGEMENT WITHIN DYNAMICS 365 FOR FINANCE & OPERATIONS
MODULE 5: CONFIGURING BATCH AND SERIALIZED PRODUCTS

Creating a Serial Tracked Product

How to do it...

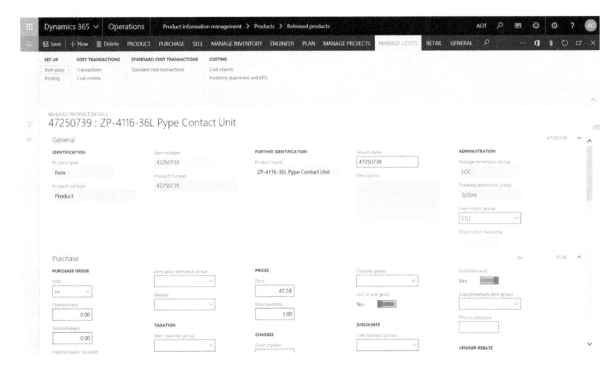

Step 17: Click Item price

Now that we have a purchase cost we will want to perform a cost rollup.

To do this just click on the **Item price** button.

dync
www.dynamicscompanions.com
Dynamics Companions

- 98 -

www.blindsquirrelpublishing.com
© 2019 Blind Squirrel Publishing, LLC , All Rights Reserved

BLIND SQUIRREL
PUBLISHING

DYNAMICS COMPANIONS
BARE BONES CONFIGURATION GUIDE

CONFIGURING INVENTORY MANAGEMENT WITHIN DYNAMICS 365 FOR FINANCE & OPERATIONS
MODULE 5: CONFIGURING BATCH AND SERIALIZED PRODUCTS

Creating a Serial Tracked Product

How to do it...

Step 18: Click Calculate item cost

When the **Item price** form is displayed we will be able ro calculate the prices from the purchase cost.

To do this just click on the **Calculate item cost** button.

www.dynamicscompanions.com
Dynamics Companions

- 99 -

www.blindsquirrelpublishing.com
© 2019 Blind Squirrel Publishing, LLC , All Rights Reserved

BLIND SQUIRREL
PUBLISHING

DYNAMICS COMPANIONS
BARE BONES CONFIGURATION GUIDE

CONFIGURING INVENTORY MANAGEMENT WITHIN DYNAMICS 365 FOR FINANCE & OPERATIONS
MODULE 5: CONFIGURING BATCH AND SERIALIZED PRODUCTS

Creating a Serial Tracked Product

How to do it...

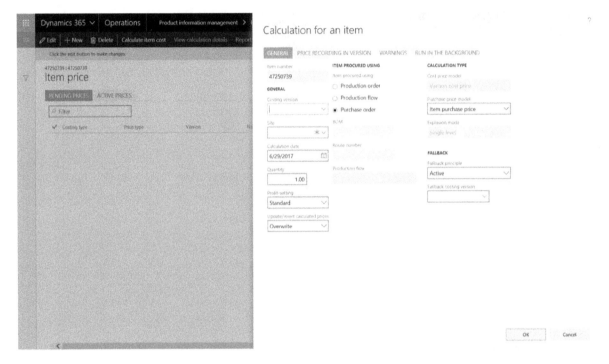

Step 18: Click Calculate item cost

This will open up the **Calculation for an item** form and we will be able to tell it what we want the cost to be associated to.

dyn c
www.dynamicscompanions.com
Dynamics Companions

- 100 -

www.blindsquirrelpublishing.com
© 2019 Blind Squirrel Publishing, LLC , All Rights Reserved

BLIND SQUIRREL
PUBLISHING

DYNAMICS COMPANIONS
BARE BONES CONFIGURATION GUIDE

CONFIGURING INVENTORY MANAGEMENT WITHIN DYNAMICS 365 FOR FINANCE & OPERATIONS
MODULE 5: CONFIGURING BATCH AND SERIALIZED PRODUCTS

Creating a Serial Tracked Product

How to do it...

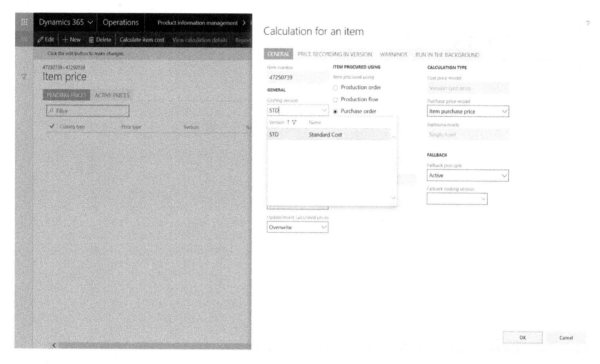

Step 19: Select the Costing version

We will start by selecting the costing version that we want the cost to be linked to.

To do this we will just need to select the **Costing version** from the dropdown list.

For this example, we will want to click on the **Costing version** dropdown list and select **STD**.

dync
www.dynamicscompanions.com
Dynamics Companions

- 101 -

www.blindsquirrelpublishing.com
© 2019 Blind Squirrel Publishing, LLC , All Rights Reserved

BLIND SQUIRREL
PUBLISHING

DYNAMICS COMPANIONS
BARE BONES CONFIGURATION GUIDE

CONFIGURING INVENTORY MANAGEMENT WITHIN DYNAMICS 365 FOR FINANCE & OPERATIONS
MODULE 5: CONFIGURING BATCH AND SERIALIZED PRODUCTS

Creating a Serial Tracked Product

How to do it...

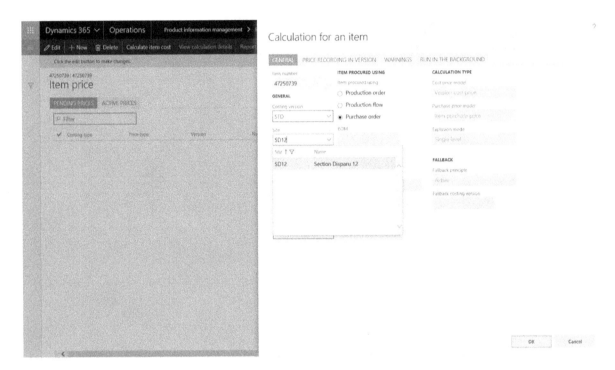

Step 20: Select the Site

And then we will select the site that we want the cost to be linked to.

To do this we will just need to select the **Site** from the dropdown list.

For this example, we will want to click on the **Site** dropdown list and select **SD12**.

dyn c   www.dynamicscompanions.com
Dynamics Companions

- 102 -

www.blindsquirrelpublishing.com
© 2019 Blind Squirrel Publishing, LLC , All Rights Reserved

BLIND SQUIRREL
PUBLISHING

DYNAMICS COMPANIONS
BARE BONES CONFIGURATION GUIDE

CONFIGURING INVENTORY MANAGEMENT WITHIN DYNAMICS 365 FOR FINANCE & OPERATIONS
MODULE 5: CONFIGURING BATCH AND SERIALIZED PRODUCTS

Creating a Serial Tracked Product

How to do it...

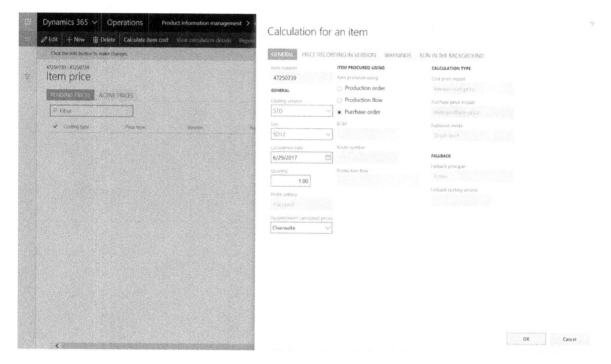

Step 21: Click OK

After we have done that we can get the system to calculate the price for us.

To do this just click on the **OK** button.

dyn c
www.dynamicscompanions.com
Dynamics Companions

- 103 -

www.blindsquirrelpublishing.com
© 2019 Blind Squirrel Publishing, LLC , All Rights Reserved

BLIND SQUIRREL
PUBLISHING

DYNAMICS COMPANIONS
BARE BONES CONFIGURATION GUIDE

CONFIGURING INVENTORY MANAGEMENT WITHIN DYNAMICS 365 FOR FINANCE & OPERATIONS
MODULE 5: CONFIGURING BATCH AND SERIALIZED PRODUCTS

Creating a Serial Tracked Product

How to do it...

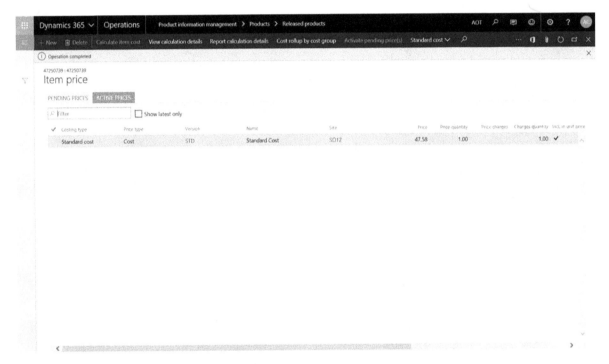

Step 22: Click Activate pending prices

When we return to the **Item prices** form we will see that the price has been calculated and we just need to activate the cost.

To do this just click on the **Activate pending prices** button.

www.dynamicscompanions.com
Dynamics Companions

- 104 -

www.blindsquirrelpublishing.com
© 2019 Blind Squirrel Publishing, LLC , All Rights Reserved

BLIND SQUIRREL
PUBLISHING

DYNAMICS COMPANIONS
BARE BONES CONFIGURATION GUIDE

CONFIGURING INVENTORY MANAGEMENT WITHIN DYNAMICS 365 FOR FINANCE & OPERATIONS
MODULE 5: CONFIGURING BATCH AND SERIALIZED PRODUCTS

Creating Serial Tracked Inventory

Now that the product is configured you can see the serial numbers in action by creating some more inventory.

How to do it...

Step 1: Click On-hand inventory

We can create the serialized inventory just the same way as we did with the batch tracked inventory.

To do this just click on the **On-hand inventory** button.

Step 2: Click Quantity adjustment

When the **On-hand** form is displayed, we can create some inventory just by doing a quantity adjustment.

To do this just click on the **Quantity adjustment** button.

Step 3: Click New

When the counting form is displayed we just create a new count line which we will use for the serialized product.

To do this just click on the **New** button.

We will

This will create a new count line for us.

Step 4: Select the Site, select the Warehouse, select the Location, update the Quantity and click OK

All we need to do is specify the inventory location dimensions and also how much of the product we are going to create.

To do this we will just need to select the **Site** from the dropdown list, select the **Warehouse** from the dropdown list, select the **Location** from the dropdown list, update the **Quantity** value and click on the **OK** button.

For this example, we will want to click on the **Site** dropdown list and select **SD12**, click on the **Warehouse** dropdown list and select **120**, click on the **Location** dropdown list and select **01-01-1**, set the **Quantity** to **10**.

When you return back to the **On Hand** inquiry you will see that 10 serial numbers have been automatically created for you.

dync
www.dynamicscompanions.com
Dynamics Companions

- 105 -

www.blindsquirrelpublishing.com
© 2019 Blind Squirrel Publishing, LLC , All Rights Reserved

BLIND SQUIRREL
PUBLISHING

DYNAMICS COMPANIONS
BARE BONES CONFIGURATION GUIDE

CONFIGURING INVENTORY MANAGEMENT WITHIN DYNAMICS 365 FOR FINANCE & OPERATIONS
MODULE 5: CONFIGURING BATCH AND SERIALIZED PRODUCTS

Creating Serial Tracked Inventory

How to do it...

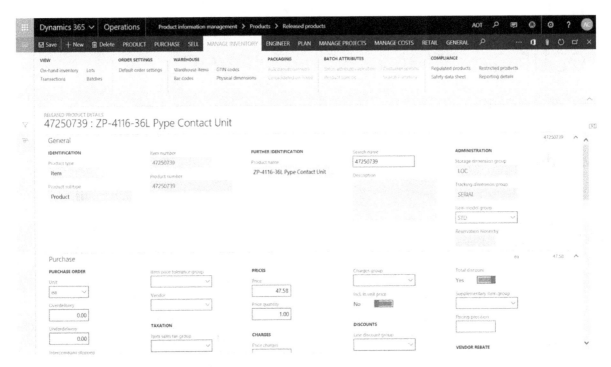

Step 1: Click On-hand inventory

We can create the serialized inventory just the same way as we did with the batch tracked inventory.

To do this just click on the **On-hand inventory** button.

www.dynamicscompanions.com
Dynamics Companions

- 106 -

www.blindsquirrelpublishing.com
© 2019 Blind Squirrel Publishing, LLC, All Rights Reserved

BLIND SQUIRREL
PUBLISHING

DYNAMICS COMPANIONS
BARE BONES CONFIGURATION GUIDE

CONFIGURING INVENTORY MANAGEMENT WITHIN DYNAMICS 365 FOR FINANCE & OPERATIONS
MODULE 5: CONFIGURING BATCH AND SERIALIZED PRODUCTS

Creating Serial Tracked Inventory

How to do it...

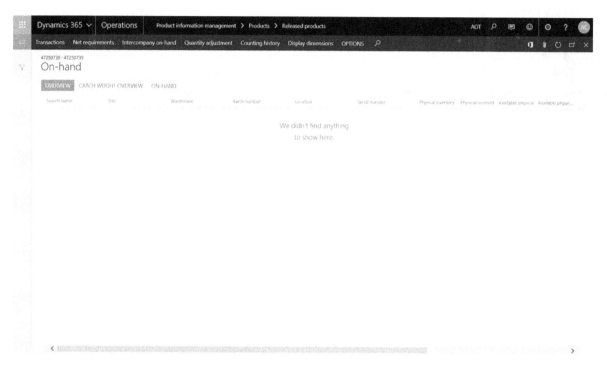

Step 2: Click Quantity adjustment

When the **On-hand** form is displayed, we can create some inventory just by doing a quantity adjustment.

To do this just click on the **Quantity adjustment** button.

dync
www.dynamicscompanions.com
Dynamics Companions

- 107 -

www.blindsquirrelpublishing.com
© 2019 Blind Squirrel Publishing, LLC , All Rights Reserved

BLIND SQUIRREL
PUBLISHING

DYNAMICS COMPANIONS
BARE BONES CONFIGURATION GUIDE

CONFIGURING INVENTORY MANAGEMENT WITHIN DYNAMICS 365 FOR FINANCE & OPERATIONS
MODULE 5: CONFIGURING BATCH AND SERIALIZED PRODUCTS

Creating Serial Tracked Inventory

How to do it...

Step 3: Click New

When the counting form is displayed we just create a new count line which we will use for the serialized product.

To do this just click on the **New** button.

dync
www.dynamicscompanions.com
Dynamics Companions

- 108 -

www.blindsquirrelpublishing.com
© 2019 Blind Squirrel Publishing, LLC , All Rights Reserved

BLIND SQUIRREL
PUBLISHING

DYNAMICS COMPANIONS
BARE BONES CONFIGURATION GUIDE

CONFIGURING INVENTORY MANAGEMENT WITHIN DYNAMICS 365 FOR FINANCE & OPERATIONS
MODULE 5: CONFIGURING BATCH AND SERIALIZED PRODUCTS

Creating Serial Tracked Inventory

How to do it...

Step 3: Click New

We will

This will create a new count line for us.

DYNAMICS COMPANIONS
BARE BONES CONFIGURATION GUIDE

CONFIGURING INVENTORY MANAGEMENT WITHIN DYNAMICS 365 FOR FINANCE & OPERATIONS
MODULE 5: CONFIGURING BATCH AND SERIALIZED PRODUCTS

Creating Serial Tracked Inventory

How to do it...

Step 4: Select the Site, select the Warehouse, select the Location, update the Quantity and click OK

All we need to do is specify the inventory location dimensions and also how much of the product we are going to create.

To do this we will just need to select the **Site** from the dropdown list, select the **Warehouse** from the dropdown list, select the **Location** from the dropdown list, update the **Quantity** value and click on the **OK** button.

For this example, we will want to click on the **Site** dropdown list and select **SD12**, click on the **Warehouse** dropdown list and select **120**, click on the **Location** dropdown list and select **01-01-1**, set the **Quantity** to **10**.

www.dynamicscompanions.com
Dynamics Companions

- 110 -

www.blindsquirrelpublishing.com
© 2019 Blind Squirrel Publishing, LLC, All Rights Reserved

BLIND SQUIRREL
PUBLISHING

DYNAMICS COMPANIONS
BARE BONES CONFIGURATION GUIDE

CONFIGURING INVENTORY MANAGEMENT WITHIN DYNAMICS 365 FOR FINANCE & OPERATIONS
MODULE 5: CONFIGURING BATCH AND SERIALIZED PRODUCTS

Creating Serial Tracked Inventory

How to do it...

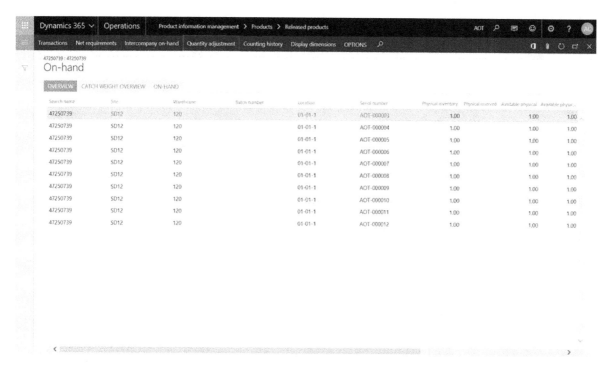

Step 4: Select the Site, select the Warehouse, select the Location, update the Quantity and click OK

When you return back to the **On Hand** inquiry you will see that 10 serial numbers have been automatically created for you.

www.dynamicscompanions.com
Dynamics Companions

- 111 -

www.blindsquirrelpublishing.com
© 2019 Blind Squirrel Publishing, LLC , All Rights Reserved

BLIND SQUIRREL
PUBLISHING

DYNAMICS COMPANIONS
BARE BONES CONFIGURATION GUIDE

CONFIGURING INVENTORY MANAGEMENT WITHIN DYNAMICS 365 FOR FINANCE & OPERATIONS
MODULE 5: CONFIGURING BATCH AND SERIALIZED PRODUCTS

Creating Serial Tracked Inventory

Review

How easy is that. Now as any product is created for this product within the system, it will create unique serial numbers for each unit automatically.

www.dynamicscompanions.com
Dynamics Companions

- 112 -

www.blindsquirrelpublishing.com
© 2019 Blind Squirrel Publishing, LLC , All Rights Reserved

BLIND SQUIRREL
PUBLISHING

DYNAMICS COMPANIONS
BARE BONES CONFIGURATION GUIDE

CONFIGURING INVENTORY MANAGEMENT WITHIN DYNAMICS 365 FOR FINANCE & OPERATIONS
MODULE 5: CONFIGURING BATCH AND SERIALIZED PRODUCTS

Conculsion

Congratulations on creating your first batch and serialized products. They are very similar to the creation of the normal products that we did earlier on, except for the additional number tracking groups that we need to assign to them.

Not all products will be managed this way, but when you do come across them you will know how to set them up.

dync
www.dynamicscompanions.com
Dynamics Companions

- 113 -

www.blindsquirrelpublishing.com
© 2019 Blind Squirrel Publishing, LLC , All Rights Reserved

BLIND SQUIRREL
PUBLISHING

DYNAMICS COMPANIONS
BARE BONES CONFIGURATION GUIDE

CONFIGURING INVENTORY MANAGEMENT WITHIN DYNAMICS 365 FOR FINANCE & OPERATIONS
MODULE 5: CONFIGURING BATCH AND SERIALIZED PRODUCTS

About The Author

Murray Fife is an Author of over 20 books on Microsoft Dynamics including the Bare Bones Configuration Guide series. These guides comprise of over 15 books which step you through the setup and configuration of Microsoft Dynamics including Finance, Operations, Human Resources, Production, Service Management, and Project Accounting.

Throughout his 25+ years of experience in the software industry he has worked in many different roles during his career, including as a developer, an implementation consultant, a trainer and a demo guy within the partner channel which gives him a great understanding of the requirements for both customers and partners perspective.

If you are interested in contacting Murray or want to follow his blogs and posts then here is all of his contact information:

Email: murray@murrayfife.com

Twitter: @murrayfife
Facebook: facebook.com/murraycfife
Google: google.com/+murrayfife
LinkedIn: linkedin.com/in/murrayfife

Blog: atinkerersnotebook.com
Slideshare: slideshare.net/murrayfife
Amazon: amazon.com/author/murrayfife

www.dynamicscompanions.com
Dynamics Companions

- 114 -

www.blindsquirrelpublishing.com
© 2019 Blind Squirrel Publishing, LLC, All Rights Reserved

BLIND SQUIRREL
PUBLISHING

DYNAMICS COMPANIONS
BARE BONES CONFIGURATION GUIDE

CONFIGURING INVENTORY MANAGEMENT WITHIN DYNAMICS 365 FOR FINANCE & OPERATIONS
MODULE 5: CONFIGURING BATCH AND SERIALIZED PRODUCTS

Need More Help with Microsoft Dynamics AX 2012 or Dynamics 365 for Operations

We are firm believers that Microsoft Dynamics AX 2012 or Dynamics 365 is not a hard product to learn, but the problem is where do you start. Which is why we developed the Bare Bones Configuration Guides. The aim of this series is to step you though the configuration of Microsoft Dynamics from a blank system, and then step you through the setup of all of the core modules within Microsoft Dynamics. We start with the setup of a base system, then move on to the financial, distribution, and operations modules.

Each book builds upon the previous ones, and by the time you have worked through all of the guides then you will have completely configured a simple (but functional) Microsoft Dynamics instance. To make it even more worthwhile you will have a far better understanding of Microsoft Dynamics and also how everything fits together.

As of now there are 16 guides in this series broken out as follows:

- Configuring a Training Environment
- Configuring an Organization
- Configuring the General Ledger
- Configuring Cash and Bank Management
- Configuring Accounts Receivable
- Configuring Accounts Payable
- Configuring Product Information Management
- Configuring Inventory Management

- Configuring Procurement and Sourcing
- Configuring Sales Order Management
- Configuring Human Resource Management
- Configuring Project Management and Accounting
- Configuring Production Control
- Configuring Sales and Marketing
- Configuring Service Management
- Configuring Warehouse Management

Although you can get each of these guides individually, and we think that each one is a great Visual resources to step you through each of the particular modules, for those of you that want to take full advantage of the series, you will want to start from the beginning and work through them one by one. After you have done that you would have done people told me was impossible for one persons to do, and that is to configure all of the core modules within Microsoft Dynamics.

If you are interested in finding out more about the series and also view all of the details including topics covered within the module, then browse to the Bare Bones Configuration Guide landing page on the Microsoft Dynamics Companions website. You will find all of the details, and also downloadable resources that help you with the setup of Microsoft Dynamics. Here is the full link: http://www.dynamicscompanions.com

dync   www.dynamicscompanions.com
Dynamics Companions

- 115 -

www.blindsquirrelpublishing.com
© 2019 Blind Squirrel Publishing, LLC, All Rights Reserved

BLIND SQUIRREL
PUBLISHING